305.42
coN
Store

:A Health and Welfa

Choice in Welfare No.

reinput 19/11/04

Free-Market Feminism

Dav.

Commentaries by

Brenda Almond
Miriam E. David
Janet Radcliffe Richards
Christina Hoff Sommers

IEA Health and Welfare Unit
London

First published April 1998

The IEA Health and Welfare Unit
2 Lord North St
London SW1P 3LB

ISBN 0-255 36435-0
ISSN 1362-9565

Typeset by the IEA Health and Welfare Unit
in Bookman 10 point
Printed in Great Britain by
St Edmundsbury Press
Blenheim Industrial Park, Newmarket Road
Bury St Edmunds, Suffolk IP33 3TU

Contents

The Authors

David Conway is Professor of Philosophy at Middlesex University where he runs a Centre for Practical Philosophy. His publications include *A Farewell to Marx*, 1987 and *Classical Liberalism: The Unvanquished Ideal*, 1995.

Brenda Almond is Professor of Moral and Social Philosophy at the University of Hull. She is President of the Society for Applied Philosophy and Joint Editor of the *Journal of Applied Philosophy*. As well as articles and reviews on a wide range of topics, she is the author of several books, including *Exploring Ethics: A Traveller's Tale*, (Blackwell, 1998); *Exploring Philosophy: Second Edition, the Philosophical Quest*, (Blackwell, 1995) and, as Brenda Cohen, *Education and the Individual*.

Miriam E. David, is Professor and Dean of Research at the London Institute. Previously she was Professor of Social Sciences and Director of the Social Sciences Research Centre at South Bank University, London. She has recently served on the Higher Education Funding Council's (HEFCE) Research Assessment Exercise (RAE) sociology panel. Her recent publications include *Mother's Intuition? Choosing Secondary Schools*, with Anne West and Jane Ribbens, 1994 and *Educational Reforms and Gender Equality in Schools*, with Madeleine Arnot and Gaby Weiner, 1996. She is co-editor, with Dr Dulcie Groves, of *The Journal of Social Policy* and an executive editor of the *British Journal of the Sociology of Education*.

Janet Radcliffe Richards is Lecturer in Philosophy at the Open University. She is the author of *The Sceptical Feminist: A Philisophical Enquiry*, RKP 1980 and Penguin 1982; Second Edition Penguin 1994. Her most recent publication on feminism is 'Why feminist epistemology isn't', in *The Flight from Science and Reason*, Gross, Levitt and Lewis (eds.), Johns Hopkins, 1997. Other recent publications are on equality of opportunity, euthanasia, and the sale of organs for transplant.

Christina Hoff Sommers is the W.H. Brady Fellow at the American Enterprise Institute in Washington DC. She has been a professor of philosophy at Clark University since 1980. Professor Sommers is best known for her writings on moral education in the schools and on the impact of feminism on American culture. She has edited a textbook in moral philosophy entitled *Vice and Virtue in Everyday Life*, which is widely used in university courses, and is the author of *Who Stole Feminism? How Women Have Betrayed Women*. She has written many articles, both for newspapers and for scholarly journals such as *The New England Journal of Medicine* and the *Journal of Philosophy*.

Foreword

In *Free-Market Feminism* David Conway argues that 1960s feminism is a corrupted version of earlier feminist traditions. In particular, earlier feminism was compatible with a society of free and responsible individuals, whereas 1960s feminism is not.

'Give everyone a chance!' was the traditional demand of liberals. They believed that there should be no artificial barriers to the advancement of talent, which meant that women should be able to compete on merit with men. Corrupted 1960s feminism, however, does not call for the removal of barriers to allow talent to find its outlet, it seeks to invent and impose barriers. Instead of calling for each to be given a chance in order to encourage responsibility and the improvements that result from the free flowering of talent, corrupted feminism has become a rationale for suppressing talent by the imposition of quotas.

1960s mind-set feminism seems to appeal to the ideal of a society open to the talents, but in reality demands equal outcomes. The result has been that, just as the older economic rationales for state centralism have been defeated, 1960s feminism has added a new one.

In keeping with many other IEA books on controversial subjects, and to add to its value as a teaching aid, Professor Conway's essay is accompanied by four commentaries. Professor Brenda Almond and Professor Chistina Hoff Sommers are broadly sympathetic to his argument, while Professor Miriam David and Janet Radcliffe Richards strongly disagree.

David G. Green

Acknowledgements

This essay was originally commissioned by the Liberales Institut (Liberty Institute) of the Friedrich-Naumann-Stiftung, Bonn. The author is grateful to the Liberales Institut for permission to publish an English-language edition of it.

The author would also like to take the opportunity to express thanks to the three anonymous referees who provided constructive criticism which helped to clarify and improve the argument. Thanks are also due to David Green and Robert Whelan of the IEA Health and Welfare Unit for their helpful suggestions.

Additionally, the author would like to thank Caroline Quest who, through innumerable conversations with him on the issues treated in this book, has greatly helped him in forming his present understanding of the subject.

Free-Market Feminism

David Conway

Summary

1 The modern form of feminism that emerged in the 1960s in the wake of the American civil rights movement differs from its nineteenth century predecessor primarily by denying that according women equal civil, political and economic rights suffices to provide them with equal opportunity to participate in the extra-domestic life of their societies.

2 To create such equal opportunity, modern feminism advocates—and has largely been successful in having had enacted —a range of further measures all of which go beyond according women the same rights as men and involve curtailing the free market in some way.

3 The main such anti-market measures advocated by modern feminism are anti-discrimination laws, affirmative action, equal pay for work of equal value, and state-provided or subsidised childcare.

4 None of these measures is necessary or effective as a means of achieving equal opportunity, and each is positively detrimental to the interests of women.

5 Anti-discrimination laws are unnecessary in a free market to eliminate discrimination against women in the workplace. Where sex is not a genuine job-related qualification, sexual discrimination places costs on employers who practise it which render them at a competitive disadvantage *vis-a-vis* those who do not. Such laws prevent employers from establishing single-sex firms in cases where economic or other benefits are to be gained from them. These laws thereby reduce the employment

opportunities of women who are as likely to benefit from single-sex firms as men.

6 To equalise the employment opportunities of women relative to men, affirmative action on behalf of women is unnecessary. The difference in the employment profiles of the two sexes is explicable in terms of factors other than past or present discrimination against women, such as their different preferences. As well as being enormously costly, affirmative action is likely to prove self-defeating through undermining the idea that women gain job advancement on merit.

7 To ensure women receive for their work all it is worth to their employers in a free market, it is not necessary to assess its worth relative to men's. This level of remuneration tends to be brought about automatically by competition between employers for labour. Attempts to raise wage rates above this level merely restrict job-opportunities, since employers have no incentives to pay such rates. As well as being neither necessary nor effective in equalising women's pay relative to men's, comparable worth encourages women to remain in traditionally female spheres of employment and thereby reduces rather than extends their employment opportunities.

8 In order for mothers of pre-school children to be able to work on equal terms with men, the state need neither provide nor subsidise childcare. For nothing compels women to have children until they and their partners can afford to make their own childcare arrangements should both partners wish to work. The costs of the state providing or subsidising childcare would so increase tax rates as to compel many women to work, even though they preferred to look after their own pre-school children at home rather than work.

9 Since women would enjoy greater and more diverse opportunities in a free market than in the regulated market advocated by modern feminists, feminists should, therefore, support rather than oppose the market.

Introduction

W HAT attitude should feminists have towards the free
market? In terms of whether it helps or hinders the
attainment of their ultimate objectives, should they look upon it
as an ally or an enemy? Or should feminists look upon the
market with indifference, as something purely neutral and
irrelevant to their aspirations? Conversely, what should be the
attitude of supporters of the free market towards feminism?
Should they regard it as friend, foe, or neutral? Should supporters of the free market view feminists as potential allies in their
cause or as among their most implacable of ideological enemies?

One could today easily be forgiven for supposing that the free
market must be inherently incompatible with the goals and
aspirations of feminism. Most contemporary feminists call for,
and, to a large extent, have achieved, the enactment of legislative
measures and policies which in both design and effect have
severely impeded the operation and workings of a free market.
These range from the legal prohibition of sex discrimination in
employment, through making mandatory equal pay for women's
work judged of equal or comparable worth to that of men, to
affirmative action in the form of quotas, goals, and reverse
discrimination, and calls for mandatory work-based state-funded
nurseries, mandatory paid paternity, as well as maternity, leave,
together with alterations in the working-day designed to accom-
modate the needs of women with children. Correspondingly, most
free marketeers are inclined today to distance themselves from
feminism and write it off as essentially and integrally anti-
capitalist in outlook.

It would, however, be over-hasty in the extreme for either party
to write off the other as inherently antagonistic to its own
favoured objectives and ideals. It is true that practically all the
different varieties of contemporary feminism, especially those
whose leading advocates command so much media attention
today, are anti-capitalist in tone and intent. However, these by no
means exhaust all the varieties of feminism. A less-well known,
but, nonetheless, entirely distinct, variety exists that is not
hostile to the free market. On the contrary, this species of
feminism regards the market, together with the other political

institutions constitutive of liberal democracy, as among the principal instruments through which the cause of female emancipation and sexual equality can be advanced. Because, among all the varieties of feminism, this one alone views the market in a favourable light, it will be referred to here as *free-market feminism*. Because virtually every other is hostile to the free market, in what follows they shall collectively be referred as *anti-market feminism*.

The leading contemporary exponents of free-market feminism are Wendy McIlroy and Joan Kennedy Taylor.[1] Another feminist who may be regarded as being broadly sympathetic to this point of view is Christina Hoff Sommers.[2] Its roots, however, can be traced back to an earlier classical liberal form of feminism. This flourished in the second half of the nineteenth century and early twentieth century.[3] Its ancestry can, in turn, be traced back still earlier to the writings of John Stuart Mill[4] and Mary Wollstonecraft.[5]

The present study aims to expound and defend free-market feminism against the tenets and anti-market nostrums shared by contemporary anti-market feminism. It will explain what is common ground, as well as what is principally at issue, between free-market and anti-market feminism. It will then examine in turn each of the principal anti-market policy measures advocated by contemporary anti-market feminism in the name of women. The principal arguments for each measure will be set out and critically examined. All will be found wanting. The free-market feminist case against each will then be stated. My principal conclusion will be that none can be justified in terms of the stated ultimate goals and objectives of feminism which, it will be argued, are far better able to be achieved through the free market.

Varieties of Feminism

No matter how much at variance with one another all the different varieties of feminism might be, if the term is to have any meaningful content at all, they must all subscribe to some common core doctrine, or set of doctrines, denied by their opponents. My immediate concern is to explain what unites, as well as what divides, those varieties of feminism favourable to the free market and those opposed to it. Before doing so, it is worth pointing out that, typically, the various individual species of feminism are designated by names which give no indication of their bearers' respective attitude towards the market. Instead, that which favours the free market is more commonly known as *classical liberal feminism* or *classical feminism* for short. Likewise, each of the distinct varieties of anti-market feminism is usually referred to by an expression formed by conjoining that general term with some qualifying adjective that connotes some main respect in which that particular species differs from other members of the genus. This results in a plethora of exotically named species such as 'radical feminism', 'socialist feminism', 'post-modern feminism', and so on.

Despite the many very real doctrinal differences between free-market and anti-market feminism, they clearly share some common ground. No matter whether their attitude towards the market is friendly or hostile, all species of feminism subscribe to some doctrine or doctrines not subscribed to by those hostile to feminism. Whatever these doctrines are, they may be said to constitute the *fundamental tenets of feminism*. For the purposes of this study, these are taken to consist of a factual claim and a closely related value-judgement. The factual claim is that, *as a result of having, from time immemorial up to and including the present, enjoyed less opportunity than men to participate in the extra-domestic life of their societies, women have enjoyed and continue to enjoy less esteem, status, power, and independence than men*. The closely associated value-judgement is that, *since women, in general, are no less deserving than men of enjoying such opportunity, all remaining obstacles to their enjoyment of it lack moral justification and should be dismantled*. No point of view deserves to be called feminist which does not subscribe, in some form or other, to both the factual claim and value-judgement No point of view is hostile to feminism, unless it rejects either the factual claim or the value-judgement, or both.

As well as subscribing to these two fundamental tenets of feminism, free-market feminism agrees with its anti-market counter-part on three further matters. There is, first, common agreement on what has been the principal way in which, historically, women have been denied equal opportunity. It is common ground that it was by their having been accorded fewer legal civil and political rights than men. Women were ineligible to vote long after men were enfranchised. They have been unable to own property in their own name, after marriage, when men were. Until comparatively recent times, they were legally compelled upon marriage to give up full-time employment, clearly something no men have been compelled to do. There is common agreement, second, that, notwithstanding having now acquired the same civil and political rights as men, women nevertheless continue to enjoy less opportunity than men to participate in the extra-domestic life of their societies. Third, all feminists agree that the principal reason why women today continue to enjoy less opportunity than men is because they are more prone than men to be discriminated against on grounds of their sex, in cases where it is not strictly relevant to whatever it is invoked to exclude them from. This can range from employment to educational opportunities.

Beyond this, agreement between free-market and anti-market feminism breaks down. It does so, principally, on two issues. The first is whether curtailment of the market is either necessary or desirable to eradicate such discrimination against women as they continue to suffer, despite having been accorded the same civil, economic, and political rights as men. All shades of anti-market feminism maintain it is both, whereas free-market feminism denies it is either.

The second issue concerns whether the continued widespread existence and acceptance of traditional sex roles, particularly with regard to parenting, itself forms any part of, or otherwise contributes to, the continuing denial to women of equal opportunity to participate in extra-domestic life. Anti-market feminists uniformly assert it does; whereas free-market feminism denies this. Among the principal ways in which, according to anti-market feminists, women continue to be denied equal opportunity today is by the perpetuation of these traditional gender-roles, especially with respect to parenting. These make women the primary carers of their small children and men their primary providers. Notwithstanding how widely accepted these roles might be in a society, so anti-market feminists maintain, their continuance is sufficient to deny women as much opportunity as men to participate in extra-domestic life and hence to acquire as much esteem, power, and independence as men. For, so the argument goes, upon having children, these roles demand that women, not men, withdraw from this sphere, wholly or at least partly, in order to look after them. It is precisely because anti-market feminists consider traditional sex roles so inherently and profoundly inimical to equal opportunity for women that so many of the anti-market measures for which they call are designed precisely to undermine or do away with these roles.

Free-market feminists take a different view of traditional sex roles. To them, their continuance on a large scale need not signify that women are being accorded any less opportunity than men to participate in extra-domestic life. Rather, their continuance on a large scale can—and, in the eyes of many free-market feminists, should—be seen to be the result of a perfectly sensible and wholly innocuous set of complementary responses on the part of the members of both sexes to a fundamental circumstance likely to affect their lives to an equal degree. This circumstance is the very strong probability each has of becoming a parent during the course of their lives, and thereupon assuming, together with their partners, the responsibility for the care and maintenance of their own children. This circumstance remains equally likely for both men and women, irrespective of what permutation is effected between them of the tasks associated with these responsibilities.

Anti-market feminists all invariably assume that the continuance of traditional sex roles is simultaneously both the historical product and major contributory cause of women's present lack of equal opportunity. In their eyes, therefore, traditional gender roles stand in need of eradication. By contrast, free-market feminists are content to regard the continuance of these roles as perfectly compatible with the enjoyment by men and women of full equality of opportunity. Traditional gender roles are judged to be compatible with equal opportunity whenever, and to the extent that, they are willingly accepted and adopted by their occupants. Unlike anti-market feminism, therefore, free-market feminism sees no need to dispute any of the mounting body of empirical evidence for the existence of deep-seated biologically-rooted motivational differences between the sexes which might lead couples to *choose* to divide their labour between them in ways which conform with traditional sex roles.[6]

In sum, two main issues divide free-market feminists from their anti-market counter parts. The first is whether restricting the free market is the best or only way to eliminate all such remaining forms of discrimination against women from which (all feminists agree) women undeservedly continue to suffer, and which (they all further agree) should be eradicated. The second is whether to include, among the principal surviving forms of sex-discrimination from which women undeservedly continue to suffer and which should be eradicated, the continuance of traditional sex roles, especially in relation to parenting.

Free-market feminists are prepared to regard it as being perfectly possible that the continuance of traditional sex roles is the result of their being spontaneously and freely chosen—or, at least, fully and freely acquiesced in—by the men and women who occupy them. Should this be so, then many of the anti-market measures advocated by anti-market feminists with the intent or effect of undermining traditional sex roles must lack warrant in relation to any of the legitimate goals of feminism. All that these goals can justify feminists in seeking to do is to remove obstacles to women's enjoying equal opportunity to participate fully in their societies. Feminism goes beyond any legitimate aspiration it might have and becomes oppressive, totalitarian, and liberty-denying, if and whenever it seeks to ensure that women avail themselves of these opportunities, regardless of whether or not they want to. Anti-market feminists do precisely this through advocating policy-measures which both in design and effect deny women the opportunity to *decline* to avail themselves of their opportunities to participate as fully as men in extra-domestic activities, out of a preference to be primarily a homemaker and carer of their children.

A related and currently highly important question—which goes beyond the debate between free-market and anti-market feminists—is whether the institutions of the free market and liberal democracy are conducive to or subversive of the continuance of traditional sex roles. This question has assumed its current importance from two facts. The first is the growing body of empirical evidence which suggests that children succeed better in life as a result of growing up within stable two-parent families than within any other milieu. The second is the increasing fragility of this family form as indicated by the unprecedentedly high and seemingly ever-mounting rates of divorce and single parent families. In the face of these facts, some have wondered whether the market, together with the other institutions constitutive of liberal democracy, offers enough support for this family form and the traditional gender-roles associated with it. Should they not do so, some have argued, curtailments to equality of opportunity between the sexes are in order for the sake of supporting this institution. Hugely important though this issue be, it is somewhat tangential to the main concern of the present study, which focuses on what is at issue between free- and anti-market feminists. Accordingly, I do not propose to address it in any detail here, having done so elsewhere.[7]

My broad contention is that, to ensure that those who have children do so within family units of a broadly traditional type, all that is necessary is the economic and social discipline that would be imposed upon couples by the market plus strictly limited government. In my view, the disturbingly high rates of marital break-down and single-parent families prevalent today have not arisen as a result of the market being somehow inimical to women's occupying their traditional nurturant roles. Rather, these trends are the result of a variety of comparatively recent state-interventions in the fields of taxation, social security, the labour market, and family policy, which have all combined to severely impede what would otherwise in a market order be a natural tendency towards the formation and continuance of strong traditional two-parent families.[8]

The Anti-market Agenda of Modern Feminism

Historically speaking, feminism has developed in two main waves. The resulting forms it has assumed in consequence of each I may call respectively *classical* and *modern*. *Classical feminism* was primarily a nineteenth century phenomenon. It sought to do away with the prevailing legal subordination of women to men. Its aim was for women to enjoy the same civil and political rights as men: rights to life, liberty, and property, and the right to vote and stand for political office. Such rights were perfectly compatible with a free market, and classical feminism was free-market in orientation.

By the time the second wave of feminism began in the mid-twentieth century, all these had, by and large, been won. *Modern feminism* still has the same ultimate objective as classical feminism. However, the conviction from which modern feminism starts is that legal equality between the sexes was by itself insufficient to bring about or permit equality of opportunity between the sexes. In the view of modern feminists, additional legislative measures are needed which, of necessity, all involve curtailing the market in some way.

Among the most influential of modern feminists in terms of helping to draw up and popularise an anti-market policy agenda are Betty Friedan and Gloria Steinem. The former was the founding-president of the National Organization of Women, the largest feminist grouping in the United States, as well as being author of a massively influential modern feminist tract, the *Feminine Mystique*.[9] The latter was the founding-editor of another highly influential feminist publication, the aptly-named magazine, *Ms.*. The following pair of quotations from their writings give succinct expression to the general sentiment which underlies modern feminism as well as a graphic hint of the anti-market brew in process of being concocted. First, Betty Friedan.

> Thanks to the early feminists, we who have mounted the second stage of the feminist revolution have grown up with the right to vote, ... with the right to higher education and to employment, and with some, not all, of the legal right to equality .... [But] even those of us who have managed to achieve a precarious success in a given field still walk as freaks in 'man's world' since every profession—politics, the church, teaching—is still structured as man's world... Women, almost too visible as sex objects in this country today, are at the same time invisible people. As the Negro was the invisible man, so women are the invisible people in America today. To be taken seriously as people, women have to share in the decisions of government, of politics, of the church—not just to cook the church supper, but to preach the sermon; not just to look up the zip codes and address the envelopes, but to make the political decisions; not just to do the housework of industry, but to make some of the executive decisions ... If we are going to address ourselves to the need for changing the social institutions that will permit women to be free and equal individuals, participating actively in their society and changing that society—with men—then we must talk in terms of what is possible, and not accept what is as what must be ... We need not accept marriage as it's currently structured with the implicit idea of man, the breadwinner, and woman, the housewife. There are many different ways we could posit marriage. To enable *all* women, not just the exceptional few, to participate in society we must confront the fact of life ... that women do give birth to children. But we must challenge the idea that a woman is primarily

responsible for raising children. Man and society have to be educated to accept their responsibility for that role as well ... If more than a very few women are to enjoy equality, we have an absolute responsibility to get serious political priority for childcare centres, to make it possible for women not to have to bow out of society for ten or fifteen years when they have children. Or else we are going to be talking of equal opportunities for a few.[10]

Much the same sentiments are expressed by Gloria Steinem in an article published in 1970 by *Time* magazine and provocatively entitled, 'What it Would be Like if Women Win'. Here she writes:

Women don't want to exchange places with men ... That is not our goal. But we do want to change the economic system to one more based on merit. In Women's Lib Utopia, there will be free access to good jobs—and decent pay for the bad ones women have been perform-ing all along, including housework ... The American child's classic problem—too much mother, too little father—would be cured by an equalisation of parental responsibility. Free nurseries, school lunches, family cafeterias built into every housing complex, service companies that will do household cleaning chores in a regular businesslike way, and more responsibility by the entire community for the children: all these will make it possible for both mother and father to work, and to have equal leisure time with children at home.[11]

These two quotations provide a revealing glimpse of what was to become the standard anti-market policy agenda of modern feminists. Above all, modern feminists have campaigned for, and, to a large extent, have been successful in getting adopted onto the statute books, four anti-market measures. It is these four measures which are the main focus of the present study. They are, first, *anti-discrimination laws*, including equal pay for equal work, second, *affirmative action*, third, *comparable worth*, more commonly known in Britain as *equal pay for work of equal value*, and, fourth, *state-provided or subsidised childcare*. Each of these four measures involves a profound curtailment of the market.

Anti-discrimination laws prohibit employers from discriminating against women on grounds of sex in hiring, promoting, and setting pay levels for personnel. Such laws, therefore, restrict the freedom of contract between employers and potential employees otherwise existent in a free market.

Affirmative action consists in employers, on pain of penalty, taking special steps to increase the recruitment and career advancement of women and other specially favoured groups, such as ethnic minorities, which they would be under no compulsion to do in a free market.

Affirmative action can take a weaker or stronger form. The weaker form is sometimes called *positive action*, the stronger *reverse* or *positive discrimination. Positive action* can assume any one or more of the following three forms. The first is so-called *aggressive outreach* which consists in firms taking special steps to draw the attention of members of some targeted group, such as women, to the existence of opportunities for appointment to positions in which, traditionally, they have been represented in smaller numbers than corresponds with their proportion of the total population. These special steps can range from placing job-advertisements in journals specially catering for members of the targeted group, such as women's magazines, to including within general job-advertisements a statement specially welcoming applications from members of the targeted group. The second main form which affirmative action can take is the mounting by employers or the government of *special training programmes*, designed exclusively for members of the targeted group, so as to qualify them better for positions in which they have traditionally been 'under-represented'. The third is the *setting and monitoring of targets with accompanying time-tables* for increasing their representation in these positions.

Positive or *reverse discrimination* consists in employers discriminating in favour of members of a targeted group, such as women, at the point of selecting candidates for job-appointments or promotion. Selection of the successful candidate is made on the basis of their being a member of a group whose increased representation and career advancement is being actively sought. By contrast, all that positive action seeks to do is increase the number of candidates from the under-represented groups putting themselves forward for selection: selection being then made solely on the basis of individual merit and without reference to considerations of group membership. Reverse discrimination occurs whenever quotas are set for members of the targeted group, or if members of the targeted group are selected for an appointment in preference to a no less well-qualified candidate who is not of that group. Whereas, in Britain, positive action on behalf of women and ethnic minorities is legally permitted and actively encouraged by the government, positive discrimination is not.

The distinction is made on the ostensible grounds of the former measure, but not the latter, being deemed compatible with equality of opportunity. Many, however, would dispute whether there is much difference between the two, since, in practice, targets tend to work like quotas, and training programmes reserved exclusively for only certain restricted groups arguably discriminate in their favour.

Comparable worth is the practice of setting the pay for certain kinds of job by means of panels of independent adjudicators assessing its worth relative to other kinds of work in terms of difficulty or social value and awarding the same pay for work of that kind as is paid for work deemed to be of comparable value or worth to it. This method of setting pay is mandatory for all employers throughout the European Union and Australia, and has been adopted for public sector employees in the American state of Minnesota. Clearly, the legal requirement for employers to determine the pay of their employees through this means amounts to a major incursion into the free market. It denies them freedom to negotiate wage levels with their employees according to their own assessments of its value to them.

State-subsidised childcare involves the state either directly providing itself, or else providing tax incentives for employers to provide for their employees' pre-school children, crèche and nursery facilities during the working day to enable mothers as well as fathers to work. As they are financed out of general taxation, such forms of childcare provision deny parents the liberty to decide for themselves, with or without the negotiated voluntary assistance of their employers, what form of provision of care to make for their children. By imposing taxes upon those who work in order to finance it, even state-subsidised childcare reduces the disposable income of those couples who might otherwise have preferred to meet their childcare needs through one of them looking after their pre-school children, with the other partner working full-time. To maintain previous levels of family income, in the face of the additional taxation exacted by the state from those who work to pay for the building and running of nurseries, both partners might become obliged to work.

Each of these four measures has been assiduously and enthusiastically campaigned for by modern feminists and has been portrayed as being necessary to enable women to enjoy equal opportunity. Anti-discrimination laws have been deemed necessary to counter-act such residual prejudice against women by employers or their customers as would otherwise lead employers to discriminate against women in recruitment or pay. Affirmative action on behalf of women has been deemed necessary to counter-act the unconscious discrimination against them said to be still rampant, as well as to counter-balance an unfair advantage in the labour-market that past discrimination against women is said to give men through resulting in women having fewer role-models and hence less self-esteem and confidence. Even with anti-discrimination laws and affirmative action in place, the labour market can still remain highly segregated according to sex, with different kinds of work continuing to be regarded by each sex as their own distinct special province. So long as such sex-segregation endures, then, so anti-market feminists argue, without further constraints upon the market, there is no way to eliminate either unconscious discrimination against women being practised by their employers or women in female jobs losing out in wage-bargaining through enjoying less confidence and assertiveness than men. To remedy these adverse effects of labour-market segregation upon women in relation to their remuneration, it is argued, something more is required of employers beyond their being obliged to pay women equal rates of pay to men for performing the same type of work. In addition, they must be required to pay women equal remuneration for work which, though different in kind to that which is typically performed by men, is deemed of comparable or equal worth. Hence, anti-market feminism demands the policy of so-called comparable pay. This removes the settlement of women's pay from the market and puts it into the hands of job-evaluation panels whose task is to ascertain its comparable worth to that performed by men. Finally, it is argued, to enable women to take their place fully alongside men, they must cease to be expected to have to combine paid employment with being the primary carers of their children. In order for women to be relieved of this expectation, working women must be provided, either by their employers or directly by the state, with subsidised childcare facilities in the form of creches or on-site nurseries, and with other amenities such as flexible working-hours, guaranteed jobs after breaks for maternity leave, and mandatory entitlement to paternity as well as maternity leave. All such measures impose further constraints upon the free market.

A free-market society is one which accords its adult members equal civil and political legal rights, including equal freedom to compete in the labour market. No one is legally excluded from being able to compete for any job on grounds of sex, race or religion. Equally, however, a free-market society is one which accords its members *freedom of contract*. Each is legally free to contract or refrain from contracting with any other member of society who wishes to contract with them, for any purpose which does not involve violating the equal rights of any unconsenting third parties. A free-market society, therefore, is one which permits overt sex-discrimination by employers both in terms of job-selection and pay. A free-market society is one which permits an employer the freedom to contract, as well as to refrain from contracting, with anyone whom the employer chooses. Thus, a free-market society permits an employer to select a man over a no less or even better qualified woman. Furthermore, provided women are willing to work on such terms, it permits an employer to pay female employees less than male employees for precisely the same job. Such forms of discrimination against women remain possible and permissible in a free-market society, even after the removal of all legal barriers to entry of women. A free market can, also, permit employers to deny women maternity leave, let alone paternity leave, and to make no concessions to employees with children. Modern feminism, therefore, is diametrically opposed to the free market.

In the case of these four anti-market measures advocated by modern feminists, I shall now explain why free-market feminism denies them to be either necessary or desirable ways for achieving equal opportunity for women.

Anti-discrimination Laws

For many people who would not otherwise consider themselves especially feminist in orientation and sympathies, no laws are more morally innocuous, moderate, and well-justified than those that prohibit sexual and racial discrimination in relation to hiring, pay-levels, and promotion. In their view, any opposition to such laws can be motivated by nothing other than sexual or racial prejudice, rather than by any genuine concern for the interest and well-being of the specific groups such legislation is designed to protect. Yet, drawing on the seminal work of Richard Epstein,[12] I will now argue below that these widely shared sentiments about such laws are mistaken. Specifically, it will be argued, first, that such laws are not innocuous but detrimental to the interests of all members of society, including those belonging to the particular groups, such as women and blacks, which the laws were enacted to help. Second, because they are not innocuous, opposition to these laws need not invariably be motivated by sexual or racial prejudice, or by still more deplorable sentiments. Rather, as in the case of free-market feminism, opposition to them can be grounded in the belief that they restrict rather than increase the employment opportunities of those whom they are specially designed to protect. In the specific case of laws designed to prohibit sexual discrimination, it shall be my intention to show how they positively reduce, rather than expand, desirable employment opportunities for women. Hence, they must be deemed incompatible with the general aim of feminism which seeks to maximise desirable employment opportunities for women. Such a set of conclusions is bound to strike many as so paradoxical that, to establish them all, it will be necessary to proceed very carefully and slowly. Let us start right at the very beginning by seeking to clarify the notion of equality of opportunity.

I have defined feminism as that movement or ideology which has as its goal or objective the creation of (maximum) equal opportunity for men and women. Specifically, feminists want women to enjoy as much opportunity as men have to participate in the extra-domestic sphere of life. By 'the extra-domestic sphere' in this context is meant the realm of paid employment. So, we may say that the common goal of all forms of feminism, of both the free- and anti-market varieties, is for women to enjoy as much opportunity as men to participate in the realm of paid work. To achieve this objective, it might be thought necessary, and anti-market feminists do suppose it necessary, that, in filling job-vacancies or in deciding whom to promote, employers must be prohibited by law from discriminating against any female candidate on grounds of her sex. Consider a job vacancy in which an employer is legally permitted to and does discriminate against a female candidate on the basis of her sex. In such an instance, that candidate cannot enjoy as much opportunity as those of the opposite sex do to be selected or promoted. Generalising from this case, it becomes easy to suppose that, in order for the employment and promotion opportunities of the two sexes to be equal and as great as possible, it is necessary for all forms of sexual discrimination in hiring and promotion to be forbidden in law, save for the important caveat where being of one particular sex can be demonstrated to be a genuine job-related qualification.

In connection with what sorts of job might the sex of a candidate be legitimately supposed to be a genuine job-related qualification? Some cases are relatively straightforward, I trust. Suppose two candidates audition for the part of Ophelia in Shakespeare's *Hamlet*, one John Doe the other Mary Roe. Assuming the production to be a conventional one and not some very *avant garde* post-modern affair, the presumption would be that being female was a genuine job-related qualification and being male a genuine disqualifier for the job. I am aware that, in Shakespeare's day, it was the convention for young boys to play the parts of females. We are not in it, and we are dealing with current productions in which the normal dramatic convention is for characters to be played by actors of the same sex as the characters. The legitimacy of the current dramatic convention of having dramatic parts of males and females played by actors of the same sex is upheld by the Sex Discrimination Act of 1975. This Act permits discrimination on grounds of sex where sex is a 'genuine occupational qualification'. The Act allows a person's sex to count as a genuine occupational qualification in selection for dramatic performance for reasons of authenticity.

This example enables us to see that, in the relevant sense of 'equality of opportunity', it is no more in this case a denial of equal opportunity for John Doe to be passed over in favour of Mary Roe on grounds of his sex than it is for Mary Roe to be passed over in favour of Helena Bonham-Carter or Helen Mirren on the grounds that, unlike either of the latter, Mary Roe cannot act her way out of a paper bag.

I am aware that, within the field of theatrical production, the current convention of casting actors and actresses in accordance with the gender of characters to be portrayed has on occasion in the past been—and, under pressure of modern feminist concerns, is today increasingly being—challenged.[13] I suggest, however, that, where an actor or actress is cast to portray the part of someone belonging to the opposite gender to themselves, this casting decision is made for the dramatic purpose of drawing to the audience's attention some point about male or female psychology or power relations, or else simply to challenge current conventions about gender roles. In all such cases, however, it still turns out that being of one particular sex is a genuine job qualification. Paradoxically, however, in such cases being of one sex is a genuine job-qualification for playing the part of someone belonging to the opposite sex! The general point, therefore, still holds true. Apart from a few unimportant exceptions (for example, being an extra in a crowd scene), the sex of an applicant to play the part of a character in some particular dramatic production is not irrelevant to their suitability for that job in the way it is in countless other cases, for example, being a computer programmer, a telephone operator, and so on.

In relation to the realm of work, equality of opportunity means only that no one seeking appointment or promotion should be excluded from consideration, save by reference to their degree of aptitude for it. Their sex or race should not serve to exclude or favour them, save in so far as it is genuinely relevant to their ability to perform the job in question. Thus, if, as in the case of playing Ophelia, the job is to play the part of a distressed Danish young lady, then being male is as genuine a disqualification for the job as is being unable to act.

Besides cases such as playing the dramatic parts of men or women, there are few jobs which are not capable of being performed equally by men and women. In all such cases, would discrimination against candidates of one sex on grounds of their sex amount to denying them equal opportunity relative to members of the opposite sex? Clearly, this is the view of supporters of anti-discrimination laws. The inference seems over-hasty. Although practically all jobs (including even the acting job of playing the part of Ophelia) are *capable* of being performed equally by men and by women, it does not follow that they are all capable of being performed equally as well by men and women. Some kinds of job might, in general, be able to be better performed by men than by women, as other types of work might, in general, be able to be better performed by women than men. Consider, for example, construction work which involves lifting heavy machines and considerable sustained physical exertion. No doubt, there are some women who would be far better able than are most men at performing this kind of work, and hence who are more suitable than any of them for appointment to carry out such tasks. Yet, it still remains true that, in general, men are better at performing this type of work than women. No doubt, some female weight-lifters can lift greater weights than can most men. This in no way casts any doubt either on the proposition that some men can lift greater weights than can any woman, or on the proposition that, in general, men can lift greater weights than women can.

Suppose that, in general, some types of work are better able to be done (or are more likely to be chosen) by men rather than women. Is the opportunity of women to engage in this type of work (at the same pay-levels as men receive for doing it) necessarily being restricted, if employers who hire personnel to perform this type of work are at liberty in law to discriminate against women, and, on the basis of this fact, some exercise that liberty? Clearly, this is thought to be so by supporters of anti-discrimination laws. However, it need not be so. It would be so, if all employers and female job applicants were unintelligent automata who simply and forever applied or passively endured a blanket veto on women on the basis of this statistical fact. But, on the more realistic assumption that the members of neither of these two groups are, then, within a free market, several other possibilities present themselves. First, those women who are as able or more able than most or any men at performing this kind of work and who wished to engage in it could offer their services at a wage lower than the going rate for men. By so reducing their price, such women would be able to off-set the reduction in demand for their services arising from the statistical fact that, in general, they are less suited for that type of work. There would, thus, no longer be any economic incentive for employers to discriminate against women in hiring and promoting, notwithstanding the fact that, statistically, they were, in general, less able than men to perform this kind of work, and employers were at liberty to discriminate against them. Provided some enterprising employers were willing to take the risk of hiring these women for this type of work, then, once engaged in it, those women who were as or more able than men would be able to demonstrate their ability, and remove any economic incentive for an employer to discriminate against them at all when it came to paying or promoting them. In the long run, therefore, the free market contains an in-built self-correcting mechanism which tends to eliminate all ill-founded discrimination against either sex in respect of hiring, pay, or promotion.

It is true that, given the liberty of employers to discriminate against women on grounds of their sex, some of the latter may, temporarily or even permanently, be adversely affected by such discrimination. This need not imply that, in the long run or in the aggregate, their employment opportunities need be any the less extensive than men's as a result of employers being at liberty to discriminate on grounds of sex. In relation to hiring and promotion, sex-discrimination is a two-edged sword that can just as easily work in favour of women as against them. For there are likely to be as many types of work for which, in general, women are more suited than men as there are types of work more suited to men than women. The employment opportunities of women are as likely to be increased as to be diminished by employers enjoying the liberty to discriminate on grounds of sex. In the same way as the employment opportunities of women are restricted by being discriminated against on grounds of sex, so they are increased by their being subject to discrimination in their favour.

Those favouring anti-discrimination laws on the grounds of their supposedly expanding employment opportunities seem guilty here of an elementary fallacy of composition. In the case of each particular token job, the employment opportunities of women with respect to it are obviously increased if, in filling a vacancy for it, an employer is prohibited from discriminating against women on grounds of their sex. From this, it is inferred that the employment opportunities of men and women are increased, if no employer is permitted to discriminate against either sex when hiring and promoting. This is a *non sequitur*. It overlooks two important facts. The first is that discrimination on grounds of sex increases the employment opportunities of one sex as well as diminishes those of the other. So that, provided that it goes both ways, women might end up enjoying as many and as favourable employment opportunities as men do when employers are at liberty to practise discrimination on grounds of sex than when they are not. Clearly, however, in each of these two cases each sex will not enjoy the identical set of employment opportunities as either it or the opposite sex enjoys in the other case. The second fact is that the number of job vacancies to be filled at any time might not be a constant in the equation, but rather dependent upon whether employers are able to discriminate on grounds of sex. Should a greater number and variety of jobs exist were employers at liberty to discriminate on grounds of sex than where they are not, it could well be that the net effect of anti-discrimination laws is to reduce rather than extend the employment opportunities of women and men. Compare: driving to work by car might enable someone who lives and works in Manhattan to get to work quicker than he or she might otherwise be able to do, were he or she the only person driving to work there. From this, however, it cannot be inferred that all who live and work in Manhattan would be able to get to work more quickly by driving there than they might otherwise be able to do. Quite the opposite might be the case!

Previously, I have argued anti-discrimination laws to be unnecessary to achieving the goal of equality of opportunity. The market has a built-in mechanism for eradicating discrimination on grounds of sex, wherever sex is not a genuine job-related qualification. I shall now argue that such laws are positively undesirable in relation to the objective of extending employment opportunities for women. This is because they reduce the number of job-opportunities available to both sexes. How might they be supposed to do this?

Free-market feminism contends that anti-discrimination laws have the unintended effect of *reducing* employment opportunities for men and women. It does so through appeal to the truth of three general propositions about work. The first is that some members of each sex prefer working exclusively alongside members of their own sex rather than alongside members of the other. This might be so, even though, in general, each sex is as well suited for performing the kind of work in question as the other. The second is that some members of each sex perform better when they work exclusively alongside members of their own sex than they do in mixed company. Again, this might be so, despite both sexes being as well suited as each other for the work in question, and neither preferring not to work alongside the other. The third is that, for whatever reason, in relation to certain specific types of service, some members of the public of both sexes prefer being served by members of one sex rather than by members of the other. The truth of each and any of these three propositions is sufficient to cause anti-discrimination laws to reduce the over-all employment opportunities for women (and for men). For having established that these laws are unnecessary to secure employment opportunities in a free market, all these laws do, if any of these three propositions is true, is to deprive men and women of the opportunity to work in establishments which discriminate on grounds of sex for perfectly legitimate and sound commercial reasons.

There is, indeed, reason to think that each of these three propositions is true. Undoubtedly, some women would prefer to work only alongside women rather than in mixed company. As a result, these women, or indeed others, might be able to work better in such circumstances. Likewise, some women and men might prefer to be served by women or men in connection with different services. For example, women might prefer women's toilets to be serviced by female toilet attendants rather than by male ones, and the converse preference might hold true of men. Equally, some men and some women might both prefer to be served by female air stewards rather than by male ones. By prohibiting employers from being able to engage in sex discrimination at the point of recruitment and pay, all these options are closed off from those people who would benefit from them. Hence, with respect to anti-discrimination laws, my conclusion must be that, not only are they unnecessary in relation to the goal of extending employment opportunities for women, they may well be positively counter-productive in achieving that objective. A free market might well be able to provide women with greater employment opportunities than anti-discrimination laws would be able to achieve for them.

Affirmative Action

While free-market feminists contend that anti-discrimination laws go beyond what the law can and should be used for to promote equality of opportunity for the two sexes, anti-market feminists complain that these laws do not go far enough. In addition to being used to prohibit employers from discriminating against women on grounds of their sex, so they argue, the law must be made to compel them actively to recruit women and advance their careers. Thus, modern feminism has come to endorse and become the most vociferous champion of that whole range of measures collectively known as affirmative action.

The grounds offered on behalf of this range of measures are several. I shall first rehearse and then subject to critical scrutiny the main argument on behalf of them. My verdict shall be that this argument does not provide a compelling case for them. Having done that, I shall set out the case against such measures. Here, my object will be to show that, as advocated by anti-market feminists, affirmative action is incompatible with the goal of maximising equality of opportunity for women, as well as objectionable for other reasons.

The fundamental argument for all forms of affirmative action goes something like this. Despite women enjoying equal civil and political rights, and despite employers not being at liberty in law to discriminate against women on grounds of their sex in recruitment, pay, or promotion, women still continue to lag behind men in terms of earnings and job-status. They tend to be concentrated in low-paying part-time jobs, and are under-represented relative to men in the most prestigious and highest paying jobs in industry, the professions, and management. There is a powerful body of empirical evidence to suggest that women are no less inherently capable than men in respect of all the main high-paying and most prestigious jobs. Therefore, so it is concluded, something must be presently holding women back from advancing up career hierarchies, despite anti-discrimination laws prohibiting overt discrimination against them. It is then argued that what holds women back today is the legacy of the discrimination from which women have suffered in the past. It has led to there being fewer women today in high-status jobs to act as role models for women than are available to men, and has resulted in a general lack of self-confidence and self-esteem in today's women. Therefore, it is argued, positive action is necessary and warranted to encourage women to apply, as well as to ensure that, upon applying, they are hired and promoted to senior positions, through targets, quotas, and reverse discrimination.

This argument relies on three basic premises. The first is that the sexual discrimination from which in the past women have, undoubtedly and unjustifiably, suffered explains their comparatively poor present-day standing in the sphere of employment, relative to men, in terms of status and income. The second is that, if it does, they are entitled to redress or compensation for their comparatively poor present-day standing in the sphere of employment. The third is that, if they are, affirmative action on their behalf is the most appropriate way in which redress may be made and compensation given.

Each and every one of these premises is rejected by free-market feminism. It takes issue with the first on two counts. First, the premise tacitly assumes there to be no innate biologically-rooted motivational differences between men and women which might equally as well be able to account for their current employment profiles relative to one another. This assumption is open to dispute. A substantial and growing body of evidence suggests that, in general, men are biologically equipped with a stronger drive than women to form and ascend social hierarchies. This could well account for why, in general, in the absence of prefer-ential policies undertaken on their behalf, women tend to be represented in smaller numbers than men at the top of such hierarchies.[14] Second, even if there are no innate biological differences between men and women which can equally as well account for their respective current employment profiles, the first premise assumes there to be no possible mutual advantages in members of each sex effecting a sexual division of labour between themselves which could equally as well account for their relative employment profiles. Even in the absence of any innate biolog-ically based motivational differences between men and women, there could still be mutual advantages for members of both sexes in effecting between themselves some form of division of labour in which the men are assigned primary responsibility for bread-winning, and women primary responsibility for looking after their mutual off spring.[15]

The second premise of the argument is no less open to ques-tion. Suppose it is conceded that, had they not suffered sexual discrimination in the past, women would today enjoy the same employment profile as men. It still does not follow that present-day women are entitled to any redress or compensation because of the damage indirectly caused to them by the sexual discrimi-nation suffered by women in the past. There are primarily two reasons why this is so. First, at most, the only present-day women who can be considered eligible for redress or compensa-tion are those who personally have ended up worse off as a result of past discrimination against women. Arguably, this is by no means true of *all* present-day women. Consider, for example, the daughters of the most affluent members of present-day society, attending the best schools and possessed of every other social advantage. Can they seriously be supposed to be currently suffering any disadvantage as a result of past discrimination practised against women? If not, why should they be supposed entitled to any form of redress or compensation? Clearly, there is no reason why they should. Second, at most, the only people from whom redress or compensation may legitimately be extracted on behalf of whichever women are entitled to receive it are those who may be said to be currently better off than they would have been had there been no discrimination against women in the past. But who is to say exactly who these people are? It is not necessarily all men, by any means. Furthermore, women are by no means the *only* group to have been subjected to unwarranted discrimination in the past. Each present-day Western society is made up of a number of different ethnic or religious groups, many of which have in the past suffered historic injustices at the hands of others. Can all present-day disadvantages from which any member of any of these might currently suffer as a result of these historic wrongs to their forebears be redressed? If, as seems overwhelmingly likely, they cannot, why should those which (some) women presently suffer take precedence over all these others? If there is no reason, and if not all the present-day ill effects of historic wrongs against groups can be righted through compensation, then women today need not necessarily be entitled to any redress or compensation for any comparatively poorer standing which they might have today relative to men as a result of sexual discrimination suffered by other women in the past.

The third premise of the argument for affirmative action fares no better than the other two. Suppose it is granted that all present-day women are deserving of compensation and redress for the damage to their esteem and self-image that they have sustained as a result of centuries of past discrimination against women. Even so, it would still be open to doubt whether affirmative action is either the most equitable or effective way in which such redress is to be made. So far as its equity is concerned, affirmative action on behalf of women may be argued to be far too clumsy and indiscriminate a way in which redress is to be obtained on their behalf. Such compensation as it extracts on behalf of women is extracted solely from those male applicants who, as a result of it, are passed over in selection for jobs and promotion and who would otherwise have been appointed or promoted had the affirmative action not taken place. It is unfair that they alone, or sometimes even at all, should have to bear the costs of compensation. As such, it follows that those forms of affirmative action which do focus costs in this way are unfair.

Doubt may also be raised as to the effectiveness of affirmative action as a means of compensating women. It is arguable that, in the long run, affirmative action will prove self-defeating. Unless women are appointed and promoted solely and exclusively on the basis of merit, their achievements are always liable to be supposed both by themselves and others to be owed less to their merit than to discrimination in favour of them. This is hardly likely to do much to enhance their self-esteem or their standing in the eyes of men, many of whom who will be liable to harbour resentment towards women through rightly or wrongly supposing themselves to have been or vulnerable to being passed over in favour of no better qualified women as a result of such action. In sum, the modern feminist case for affirmative action is profoundly flawed.

If there are no good reasons in favour of affirmative action on behalf of women, there is, however, no shortage of good reasons against such action. One reason is that just given: *viz.* that, in the long run, it is liable to prove counter-productive as a way of improving the employment and promotion prospects of women. Another is that the huge economic costs involved in making affirmative action mandatory on any large-scale are likely to reduce the employment opportunities of both men and women. It has been estimated that, in the United States, where, admittedly, affirmative action has been made mandatory on behalf of racial minorities as well as women, gross national product has been depressed by as much as four per cent.[16] This sum is equal to the entire cost of the US state school system.

The costs of affirmative action have several distinct components. There are, first, the so-called *direct costs of compliance.* These comprise both the costs of maintaining the regulatory bodies as well as the expenditure incurred by firms in proving compliance, as well as in complying with mandatory procedures, that is form-filling as well as, for example, placing special advertisements for jobs. Second, there are the so-called *indirect costs* which consist of the time and overheads that firms must divert from normal activities to compliance. Third, and not least, there are the *opportunity costs*. These consist of the wealth that could have been created had the more tangible costs been devoted to production rather than to affirmative action. The primary opportunity costs of affirmative action are the research, design and modernisation that must be foregone in order for it to be carried out. Finally, among the costs of affirmative action must also be included the inferior economic performance of whoever gains any appointment or promotion through reverse discrimination being exercised in favour of their sex rather than their being the candidate best qualified for the job. Given all these costs, it is arguable that women are net losers rather than net beneficiaries of affirmative action undertaken on their behalf. This is especially so in view of the considerable evidence which suggests that women have not appreciably become helped by it to improve their relative position in the sphere of work. Such improvement as has occurred could well have done so, quite independently of affirmative action—indeed, in spite rather than because of it.[17]

Notwithstanding any improvement that may or may not have occurred in recent times in women's employment standing relative to that of men, the fact remains that most working women still tend to be congregated within a small number of different kinds of job which tend to be performed primarily by women and to be less well remunerated than the kinds of job primarily performed by men. In the face of these facts, many modern feminists have advocated, and have managed to have adopted onto statute books, a further anti-market measure besides anti-discrimination laws and affirmative action. This measure is so-called *comparable worth* or, as it is more commonly known in the United Kingdom, *equal pay for work of equal value*. It is to a consideration of this measure I now turn.

Comparable Worth

Notwithstanding the introduction throughout the Western world of anti-discrimination laws and affirmative action, women who seek paid employment still tend to be concentrated within a limited number of kinds of work and men within certain others. More specifically, the kind of work in which women tend to concentrate is work of a nurturant sort: such as secretarial work, social work, teaching, nursing, and catering. Moreover, these kinds of job tend to be less well paid than are the jobs in which men tend to concentrate. Given these facts, many modern feminists have advocated that the rates of pay for women should not be left to ordinary market-mechanisms. Rather, they claim, women's pay should be determined according to assessments of the comparable worth of their jobs relative to mens', to be made by review bodies composed of independent 'experts'.

Advocates of this measure as a means of improving women's pay relative to that of men base their case on three assumptions which jointly are supposed to explain the indisputable facts about women's pay just mentioned. The first is that the remuneration that women receive for this kind of work tends to be far less than it can be demonstrated to be objectively worth. The second is that women tend to be concentrated in this kind of work as a result of past and present sexual discrimination against them. More specifically, advocates of comparable pay suppose women are especially encouraged to go into nurturant types of work because members of their sex are thought to be, and encouraged to think of themselves as being, peculiarly well-suited for it. They further suppose that women are encouraged to be compliant and non-competitive, so making them more susceptible than men to settling for the lower wages that employers are prone to offer them as a result of nurturance being under-valued historically because of its association with women, and of their doing it domestically and so unpaid. The third assumption is that determining the remuneration of women's work by assessing its comparable worth relative to that of men will close that part of the pay gap between the sexes attributable to the discrimination against them which women have and continue to suffer.

All these three assumptions are rejected by free-market feminism. As before, I shall first rehearse objections to each in turn, before presenting positive reasons why, in terms of their own interests, the pay of women is better determined by market forces than by reference to putative considerations of its comparable worth.[18]

The first of the three assumptions is open to two major objections. The first is, very simply, that jobs have no intrinsic worth capable of being objectively measured. Evidence that they do not comes from the fact that job evaluation schemes used to establish the comparable worth of women's jobs are notoriously riddled with subjectivity and arbitrariness. Two actual illustrative examples may be cited in support of this claim. The first relates to the assessments made of the same range of jobs by different panels of job evaluators acting for three different American states.

> While Minnesota ranked a registered nurse, a chemist, and a social worker equally, Iowa found the nurse worth 29 per cent more than the social worker, who in turn was worth 29 per cent more than the chemist. Vermont reversed these ratings, paying the social worker 10 per cent more than the nurse, who was paid 10 per cent above the chemist.[19]

The second example relates to the state of Washington. When two different firms of consultants were brought in there to assess the comparable worth of different jobs,

> the first firm found discrimination that would require millions of dollars to remedy, the second found *no* disparity in pay per point salaries between predominantly male and female jobs.[20]

The first assumption is also open to question on the grounds of there being no reason to suppose that, were women to receive for the kinds of work in which they tend to concentrate less than its full economic value to their employers, they would not tend to move into other non-traditional lines of work, where it would receive its full value, until a labour shortage in the lines of work traditionally performed by women caused pay to rise there to the level of its full economic value. In short, there is no reason to suppose that, in a free market, the pay rates of women would not be subject to exactly the same set of determinants as those which apply to men's work, so that women received its full market value.

The second assumption made by advocates of comparable worth is that women tend to be concentrated in insufficiently well-remunerated forms of nurturing work because of past and present sexual discrimination against them. This assumption overlooks alternative possible, and, arguably, more plausible, explanations, both for where they tend to concentrate as well as for it tending to be lower paid than men's work. For example, women have traditionally been primary carers of their children. As a result, they have tended to choose forms of paid employment easier to combine with childcare, for example, by involving fewer hours or by being easier to exit from and return to. Hence, they have tended to cluster in the nurturant kinds of work in which they have because it is less subject than other forms of work to becoming obsolescent during their temporary periods of withdrawal from the labour market.

A second alternative possible explanation of the wage gap between men and women's work is men being, in general, more motivated than women to assume positions of leadership and to strive for monetary reward, women being more concerned than men about working conditions or rewarding inter-personal aspects of their work. It is this difference which may account for the concentration of women in a comparatively restricted number of nurturant jobs. The resulting relative over-supply of labour in these kinds of work would then drive down wage levels for them.

No less open to question is the third assumption which lies behind advocacy of comparable worth. This, to repeat, is that it alone can be effective in closing that part of the pay gap between men and women attributable to discrimination against women. First, it would appear that resort to comparable pay is neither necessary nor sufficient to close any part of the gap. Recent pay trends in the United States suggest comparable pay is not necessary to close the pay gap. There, without benefit of comparable pay,

> normal market processes ... have cut the full-time weekly pay gap from 64.6 per cent in 1981 to 74 per cent in 1991. This rate of progress is far better than that of Australia (no change) or that of the United Kingdom (a closing of the gap from 65.1 per cent to 69.7 per cent) over this approximate time frame.[21]

Nor does setting women's pay by comparable worth appear sufficient to close the gap. In the United Kingdom, its introduction did nothing to accelerate the rate at which the gap between men's and women's pay was closing prior to its introduction.[22]

Second, since the assessments made by job-evaluation panels are notoriously subjective and arbitrary, comparable worth cannot provide any reliable way of determining what part of the pay gap between the sexes is attributable to discrimination against women. Consider how comparable worth has operated in Minnesota where it has been introduced on a large-scale.

> Localities that have turned to the top consulting firms for assistance have never gotten objective job evaluation results though they have often obtained bizarre ones. Police lieutenants have been rated higher than police chiefs; utility and library directors have come out ahead of city managers; workers previously paid equally for doing equal work have been assigned unequal pay for their equal work. The workers who have fared best in the comparable-worth process have not gained because of objective measurement of job value according to objectively determined criteria. Not even the consultants think that their methods are objective. There is no agreement on factors to be included, on how they should be weighed, on even how factors such as working conditions should be measured once decided upon. In Minnesota some of the biggest gainers from job evaluation were those who were prepared, who had articulate, forceful representatives on the commit-tees, and who were skilful and assiduous in filling out the question-naires.[23]

It is clear that the real object of comparable pay schemes is not pay according to objective criteria of job evaluation. It is rather more pay for women for work they do, both absolutely and relatively to men. So far as this objective is concerned, free-market feminism maintains that comparable worth is not as effective an instrument for improving women's pay than is reliance on the market. The reasons for this are several. First, in so far as it was effective, comparable worth would be liable to over-price women's work and thereby reduce the overall number of jobs available to women, in much the same way as does setting minimum wages above market-clearing rates. When pay rates are too high, employers substitute capital for labour: secretaries are relaced by office-technology. Second, comparable worth would exacerbate sex segregation in employment. This is because it provides an incentive for women to remain in traditionally female occupations, rather than move into areas traditionally dominated by men. Third, comparable worth would indirectly disadvantage those women who venture into previously male-dominated professions, since it leads to reductions in their pay relative to those of women in traditionally female jobs. Finally, on the assumption that, in general, women are less aggressive and hierarchically motivated than men and care less than men about money and conflict, there is reason to think women will suffer if comparable worth is widely adopted to determine pay. This is because men will fight harder than women for pay increases by means of it. Since, in the absence of objective criteria, the outcome tends to be determined by political clout, it may be presumed that men would do better than women were pay extensively determined by means of comparable worth procedures. In sum, comparable worth seems to be an inappropriate way in which feminists should strive to achieve their goal of equalising the extra-domestic opportunities of women.

'But' it will be said 'if you are right about the causes of the pay gap between men and women and of the labour market segregation lying behind it, then, ultimately what prevents women from enjoying equal opportunity with men is their being expected to assume greater responsibility than men are for the care of their children. To achieve such equality of opportunity, what is wanted is that women be relieved of the expectation of having to bear greater responsibility for childcare than men'. Hence, I arrive at the final anti-market policy measure advocated by modern feminists. This is the call for the state itself to provide, or to require and provide subsidy for firms to provide on-site childcare facilities enabling mothers as well as fathers to work full-time. It is to a consideration of this fourth anti-market measure I now turn.

State-subsidised Childcare

Consider the following quotation.

[S]ubstantial inequalities between the sexes still exist in our society ... Underlying and intertwined with all these inequalities is the unequal distribution of the unpaid labour of the family. An equal sharing between the sexes of family responsibilities, especially childcare, is 'the great revolution that has not happened' ... The typical practices of family life ... are not just. Both the expectation and the experience of the division of labour by sex makes women vulnerable ... Central to this socially created inequality are two commonly made but inconsistent presumptions: that women are primarily responsible for the rearing of children; and that serious and committed members of the work force ... do not have primary responsibility, or even shared responsibility, for the rearing of children ... These are not matters of natural necessity ... Surely nothing in our natures dictates that men should not be equal participants in the rearing of their children. Nothing in the nature of work makes it impossible to adjust it to the fact that people are parents as well as workers ... Equality of opportunity ... for women ... is seriously undermined by the current gender injustices of our society ... In a just society, the structure and practices of families must afford women the same opportunities as men to develop their capacities, to participate in political power, to influence social choices, and to be economically as well as physically secure ... Much of what needs to be done to end the inequalities of gender ... will also help to equalize opportunity from one family to another. Subsidized, high-quality day care is obviously one such thing; another is the adaptation of the workplace to the needs of parents.[24]

This quotation comes from Susan Moller Okin, a prominent feminist writer. Elsewhere in the same book, she sets out more fully what set of policies she has in mind for securing equality of opportunity for women. She writes:

Public policies and laws should generally assume no social differentiation of the sexes. Shared parental responsibility for childcare would be both assumed and facilitated ... While high-quality day care, subsidized so as to be equally available to all children, certainly constitutes an important part of the response that society should make to provide justice for women ..., it is only one part ... Employers must be required by law... [to make available] parental leave during the postbirth months ... to mothers and fathers on the same terms, to facilitate shared parenting ... Large-scale employers should also be required to provide high-quality on-site day care for children from infancy up to school age. And to ensure equal quality of day care for all young children, *direct government subsidies* (not tax credits, which benefit the better-off) should make up the difference between the cost of high-quality day care and what less well paid parents could reasonably be expected to pay ... Finally, schools should be required to provide high-quality after-school programs, where children can play safely, do their homework, or participate in creative activities.[25]

A similar analysis and set of policy prescriptions are advanced by James Sterba who observes as follows:

[D]iscrimination in personal relations is the most entrenched of all forms of discrimination against women. It primarily manifests itself in traditional family structures in which the woman is responsible for domestic work and childcare and the man's task is 'to protect against the outside world and to show how to meet this world successfully' ... It is just not the case that all the basic needs of most women in technologically advanced societies are being met. Most obviously, their basic needs for self-development are still not being met ... In effect, ... [they] are still being treated as second-class persons, no matter how well-fed, well-clothed, well-housed they happen to be. This is why there must be a radical restructuring of social institutions ... if women's basic needs for self-development are to be met ... [F]amilies with preschool children require day care facilities if their adult members are to pursue their careers ... To truly share child-rearing within the family what is needed is flexible (typically part-time) work schedules ... [T]he option of flexible job schedules must be guaranteed to all those with preschool children. Of course, ... [this] would place a significant restriction on the rights of employers ... [b]ut ... is grounded on a right to equal opportunity.[26]

This analysis and set of far-reaching policy prescriptions are by no means confined to the far side of the Atlantic. Compare the following passage from the writings of two British feminists, Miriam David and Caroline New:

The sort of work that women take up is always determined by the basic family responsibilities which women are forced to put first, because nobody else will take them on ... We want from the state ... the sort of preventative help which reduces the *bad* side of family privacy: the isolation of parents, their near-total responsibility and the burden that it brings, and the sexism which makes the mother *the* key parent in the family but a person of low status and little power elsewhere.[27]

At several points earlier in the discussion, I have had occasion to speculate on why women do not occupy as many of the best paid and most prestigious and powerful positions as men, and what, if anything, should be done to remedy this fact. Modern feminism has it that the fact they do not is caused by some set of obstacles preventing them from doing so. Whatever these obstacles might be, in their view, these obstacles effectively prevent women from enjoying equal opportunity to participate in the extra-domestic life of their societies. Thus, according to them, it becomes the great remaining task of feminism to identify and remove them.

According to modern feminism, women are not as well represented as men in the highest paying and most powerful and prestigious positions in society because they are victims of sex discrimination, overt or subtle, past and present. To create equality of opportunity, so they argue, all surviving forms of discrimination against them must be eradicated, as must the baneful legacy of the past discrimination from which women have suffered. And so, the anti-market policy agenda of modern feminism is born. There must be anti-discrimination laws to make it unlawful for employers to engage in sexual discrimination in hiring and promotion. There must be affirmative action to remedy the psychological damage that women continue to endure today in terms of their self-esteem and confidence in consequence of centuries of discrimination against them. Only by means of it can women acquire role models and the confidence to try for positions from which they have previously been excluded. And, where they remain concentrated in occupations associated with their traditional nurturing role, their pay must be determined by means of assessments of its comparable worth relative to that of men's . Thus, despite having been brought up to regard themselves as fitted only for such work and uncompetitive, and despite further their work having traditionally been undervalued because associated with a sex which has in general been undervalued, women can escape having foisted on them less remuneration than is their rightful due for performing it.

In considering this modern feminist explanation of the pay gap between men and women and of the labour-market segregation which lies behind it, I have been led to advance an alternative explanation of why they both exist. Rather than being the product of past or present discrimination against women, I have entertained the alternative hypothesis that these differences between men and women in the field of employment arise from a sexual division of labour between them that is both to their mutual advantage and the product of their voluntary adoption, or at least perfectly willing acquiescence. Men and women divide their labour so that the latter bear prime responsibility for caring for their children and household, and the former prime responsibility for earning income. The existence of this sexual division of labour is, by itself, and without recourse to any postulated sex discrimination against women, sufficient to account for the differences between them in jobs and pay. No recourse to discrimination against women, past or present, is needed to account for these differences. So, the existence of these differences between men and women need not signify that the latter enjoy any less opportunity than the former to participate in the extra-domestic life of their societies, even should women be

found not to do so on as large a scale. It is just that, in general
and by and large, men and women *choose* to avail themselves of
their essentially similar opportunities in different but complementary ways from one another. Hence, there is no need for any
of the anti-market measures advocated by modern feminists in
order for women to be able to enjoy such equality: for, by and
large, it already exists. And, in so far as it does not yet do so, the
place where active steps should be taken to promote it is in
negotiation between couples on their mutual roles, and in the
education of girls and boys so that they are led to become fully
aware of all the possible options available to them. It is mis-
guided for equality of opportunity between the sexes to be sought
by restricting the free market which is to the advantage of neither
sex.

The free-market feminist explanation of the different employment profiles of men and women rests upon an assumption
about the sexual division of labour. This assumption is that the
sexual division of labour is the outcome of an informed voluntary
choice by those who adopt it, or, at least, that it is not something
that, on full reflection, they would not most prefer for themselves.
Should this assumption not be granted, should, that is, this form
of sexual division of labour be foisted upon women against their
will, then, in tracing the explanation of the different employment
profiles of men and women to the sexual division of labour,
especially with respect to parental responsibility, free-market
feminism will not have established that women enjoy equal
opportunity with men. For now it will turn out that they are being
discriminated against on grounds of their sex in being expected
and encouraged to be the primary carers of their children. All
else will follow from that one difference of expectation. Creation
of equal opportunity will require the eradication of this expectation and of the sexual division of labour to which it gives rise. In
its place, there will need to be instated the expectation of entirely
symmetrical parental responsibilities for men and women, so
called dual parenting, allowing women equal freedom to work
full-time as men. And, so, finally, I am led to consider the fourth
anti-market policy measure advocated by modern feminism: the
call for the state to provide or subsidise childcare for parents
with pre-school children, so as to enable their mothers, as well
as fathers, to work full-time, and for the state to compel firms to

grant paternity as well as maternity leave, so that fathers can do their full and fair, equal share of childcare, when it must be dispensed at home and not at the work-place or in school. Only then, so the argument goes, will women be able to compete on equal terms with men for jobs. Then and only then will they enjoy equality of opportunity. The question of who should provide childcare, then, is not a minor and peripheral matter, but absolutely pivotal in relation to the conduciveness or otherwise of the free market to the realisation of the aspirations and ideals of feminism.

How should free-market feminists respond to the call by such feminists as Susan Moller Okin, James Sterba, and Miriam David for state subsidised childcare and for firms to be compelled to make additional special provision for dual parenting? As in dealing with the other anti-market policy measures advocated by modern feminists, my discussion shall proceed in two stages. I shall, first, critically examine the arguments advanced on behalf of these measures and explain why they are uncompelling. Then, I shall present the case against, where I shall argue them to be inimical to the aspirations and ideals of feminism.

The first point that needs to be made is that anti-market modern feminists like Susan Okin and Miriam David have not made out a case for state-subsidised childcare and other requirements for dual parenting being thought *necessary* for supplying women with the same range of employment opportunities as men currently enjoy. Women work and acquire their sexual partners *before* they have children with them. Before they do, any couple could, if both partners chose, *decide* that, if and when they did have children, they would, quite independently of everyone else, adopt a perfectly symmetrical division of labour between themselves, involving dual parenting and equal work, whether this be full-time or part-time. Such a form of sexual division of labour, or, more accurately, such a non-division, might lead to their losing some joint income. This is because the couple would have to forgo the economic benefits that can be expected to result from their enhanced productivity brought about by the greater degree of specialisation which the division of labour makes possible. However, the decision to adopt such a form of non-division of labour between themselves would still be available to a couple in a free-market society, as would the option of their deciding that it be the father who is to assume prime responsibility for home-making and childcare and the woman prime responsibility for bread-winning.

Alternatively, if their joint income would be sufficient to bear the costs, a couple could, in a free-market society, decide to pay for full-time substitute childcare in the form of a nanny, a nursery place, or through placing their children with a professional child-minder. There seems no reason why the free market would not be able to supply as much childcare as would be needed to enable those mothers who wished it to work full-time, *if that is what they want and can afford*. As regards those couples whose joint-income or earning potential would not be enough to enable them in a market society to purchase sufficient substitute childcare to enable them both to work full-time, why, *pace* Okin, should it be supposed that the state must, or should, step in and subsidise their childcare (from the taxed income of other working couples)? Maybe couples who would desire it but cannot afford to purchase extensive childcare for their children should postpone having any children until they are in a position to afford the amount of childcare they consider optimal for them. Or else, maybe, they should be willing to compromise and settle for second-best: having children but also at the same time having to endure some unwanted childcare distributed between them as they choose best.

The modern feminist demand for state-provided or subsidised childcare strongly suggests that its advocates half suspect that the generality of women might not want to work full-time when they have small children. By proposing that childcare facilities be provided or mandated by the state, and financed from taxation, the feminists who advocate these measures are depriving women of the freedom to decide not to work full-time, or even part-time, when they have children. Rather, they are compelling them all to work, irrespective of whether this is something they want to do. This is because, if the state make childcare facilities universally available, it will have to extract the necessary resources by means of taxation on earned income. It thereby contributes towards making it harder, to the point of impossibility in some cases at the margin, for couples to get by on only one earned income. Couples will thus become obliged to work full-time (or, in the case of higher earning mothers, part-time) to pay the increased taxes needed for the funding the childcare that is not wanted by them, but which has now become necessary to enable them both to work to pay the taxes imposed to finance it!

The suspicion begins to form, therefore, that modern feminists call for universal state-subsidised or provided childcare less as a measure for creating equal opportunity for men and women than as a piece of social engineering designed to achieve a certain outcome. This suspected intended outcome is *the abolition of the traditional two-parent family unit in which mothers are the primary carers of children and fathers their primary providers*, and this outcome is intended irrespective of whether it is wanted by the generality of men and women.

'Is there any harm in that?' it might be asked. 'Why should any genuine self-respecting feminist be at all concerned about preserving for men and women the option of an institutional arrangement which is the prime seat of women's continuing subordination to men? Why should any feminist object to the creation of equality of opportunity of men and women, even if the only way it can be achieved is by denying couples the ability to configure themselves into this traditional pattern of relationship?'

I have argued above that state-subsidised childcare and the other anti-market nostrums designed to facilitate dual parenting are not necessary in order for women to enjoy equality of opportunity to participate in the extra-domestic life of their societies within a market order. That, basically, is my rebuttal of the case for these measures. I shall now argue, and this amounts to my positive case against them, that these same measures would be highly detrimental to the interests of a vast number, if not the overwhelming majority, of members of both sexes. More specifically, I shall argue that they run counter to what earlier were identified as being the ultimate aspirations and aims of feminism. These were taken to be achievement of the maximum possible equal opportunity for women. What feminists are—or, at least should be—seeking on behalf of women is for their opportunities to be extended to the maximum possible degree consistent with men enjoying as large a set of opportunities. Feminists should not be concerned to remove opportunities from women. Whether or not this is intended by their advocates, the measures presently under discussion would have the effect of denying women the opportunity to be the sole or primary carers of their children.

That these policy measures deprive women of this opportunity might, perhaps, not matter, were it not that, for many women, occupying the role of full-time mother, or at least prime carer of her children, does appear to constitute a perfectly acceptable and fulfilling option. Indeed, in the case of many women, it constitutes their most preferred option, at least until their children go to school full-time.[28] As such, *modern feminism must be deemed inimical to the interests of all those women of whose most preferred role in life it would deprive them.* It would seem that, in the guise of a moral imperative flowing from the ideal of equal opportunity, modern feminists who call for these measures are seeking to foist upon other women and society more generally what, in reality, is no more than a personal lifestyle preference of their own.

The main free-market feminist argument against state-subsidised or provided childcare is that it would deny women the opportunity to be full-time mothers, or a least primary carers, and this is something there is good reason to think many women most want to be. On the basis of extensive attitudinal surveys, it has recently been concluded that:

> The unpalatable truth [unpalatable, that is, to modern feminists] is that a substantial proportion of women still accept the sexual division of labour which sees homemaking as women's *principal* activity and income-earning as men's *principal* activity in life. This acceptance of *differentiated sex roles* underlies fundamental differences between the work orientations, labour market behaviour and life goals of men and women ... The proportion of women who accept the homemaker roles varies from half to two-thirds, depending on the precise formulation of the sexual division of labour presented to them.[29]

In this matter, it is vitally important to be aware that the traditional family in which the man is sole bread-winner and the woman sole homemaker, on the one hand, and, on the other, the alternative, totally symmetrical family, much beloved in theory by modern feminists, in which there is dual parenting and equal work by both partners, by no means together exhaust the available options from which men and women can choose. There is a third intermediate option. In this arrangement, the man has prime, not sole, responsibility for bread-winning, and the woman primary responsibility for childcare and homemaking, a role that can be and is readily combined with part-time employment. For this third type of family, an enormous amount of cross-European support has been found.

One EC Eurobarometer survey provides a unique measure of support, across Europe, for the *modern* sexual division of labour, which falls half-way between the complete equal sharing of income-earning and domestic functions to separate and parallel roles. Roughly, one-third of the EC population supported each family model. In all countries there was widespread support for all three models of the family, none receiving majority support ... Overall, a two-thirds majority of European men and women favour the idea of the working wife, and a two thirds majority also favour the wife retaining all or the major part of the domestic role ... The key contribution of this survey is that it shows, for all European countries, that people who reject the complete separation of roles for men and women do not necessarily accept egalitarian or symmetrical roles: at least half only goes as far as supporting a secondary earner role for the wife, who retains the larger share of domestic childcare work.[30]

Much the same conclusion has been reached by another recent survey of attitudes to different family formations carried out in Britain.[31] Over two hundred and twenty people from a wide variety of backgrounds and age groups were each questioned in depth on their attitudes towards various different sorts of family formation. What was discovered was that greatest support for alternative family structures besides the conventional one in which the male was prime bread-winner and women prime carer is to be found among the under-30 age group. However, support for alternative family formations falls away in favour of traditional lifestyles among both sexes after the age of 30. (Between the ages of 30 and 44, support for alternative lifestyles falls from 52 per cent to 21 per cent among men, and from 45 per cent to 39 per cent among women.) By the time people reach the age of 45, support for traditional lifestyles has become very high (76 per cent of men and 69 per cent of women favour them).

The author of the report observes that '[t]he interview and case materials ... contain much evidence of respondents changing their minds on fundamental issues as they get older, particularly as they undergo certain formative experiences. Several older people not clearly trad[itiona]l in their responses had formerly supported alternative ideas (but not *vice versa*).'[32] The author of the report concludes as follows:

In policy matters the most significant finding in this study may well be that most people do still seem to gravitate towards conventional family life, and this becomes more explicit as they raise children and move into middle age. It is clear that many women would welcome greater opportunities for involvement in non-domestic roles than was generally encouraged in traditional marriages. But this can arguably be achieved through modifying conventional marriage expectations .... It is perhaps only because we have spent so long insisting on strict gender equality that we have not turned our minds to exploring the flexibility available within the framework of ordinary marriage.

This finding fits in with what is surely the most important and least publicised finding of the latest stage of the National Child Development Study, namely that those respondents reporting the highest levels of both personal and marital satisfaction were those living in traditional families ... Levels of contentment are directly associated with mutual dependence and conventional and sexually-specific roles.[33]

The *main* free-market feminist objection to state-provided or subsidised childcare, then, is that it denies women the opportunity to be full-time mothers, or, at least, primary carers, and this is what a good many of them appear to want most to be.

A second further objection to state-subsidised childcare is that, for all the feminist talk of the need for it to be *high-quality*, to approach the level of intensity that mothers provide their own children, childcare becomes prohibitively expensive, with less costly forms being much poorer in quality than the care that mothers provide. As has been observed:

The repeated call for 'affordable, high quality, and accessible day care' is a contradiction in terms. Countries which have tried to move all mothers into the workforce and all young children into day care seem to have the greatest difficulty, given any amount of resources and effort, to provide for more than about 30 per cent (at a generous estimate) of pre-school children in public institutions of any reasonable standard. In Sweden, only 19 per cent of under-threes are in municipal nurseries and 29 per cent of under-sevens ... Over 50 per cent of under-threes receive no substitute care at all. Indeed, Sweden, Russia, and other Eastern European countries have recently moved away from the goal of universal childcare as unrealisable—not least because it is so expensive and the necessary supply of resources, in terms of trained workers, for example, is simply unobtainable.

There are prohibitive costs involved in running a good childcare centre, particularly for babies ... Writers obsessed with equal employment outcomes wax enthusiastic at the 'successes' of 'more aggressive enforcement of equal opportunities laws' and tax deductions for childcare in putting more American mothers into full time jobs. The other side of the coin, involving not only the financial crisis of the American family, but the observational account of daily life in childcare centres and at minders, goes unmentioned.

Children are entitled to a healthy, secure, consistent, loving, disciplined, nurturant, and unpressurized infancy and childhood ... It would appear to be the primary responsibility of parents to provide this ... There should be help, not penalties, for parents who want to care for their own children ... The man who financially supports the family deserves to be encouraged, not deterred, by the tax system and respected, rather than branded in ... as 'irresponsible' for being a breadwinner.[34]

My final verdict on the proposal that the state should provide or subsidise universal childcare to enable mothers to work is that it should be resisted out of concern for men, women and children. It is neither necessary for providing women with equality of opportunity, nor in their best interests or those of anyone else, save at most those feminists for whom it is a means to impose their own personal lifestyle preference on those men and women who would prefer to live otherwise.

Conclusion

Free-market feminism denies that the anti-market measures advocated by modern feminism are either necessary for or effective in promoting equality of opportunity. Instead, in its view, these measures are both costly, ineffective, and deprive women of the opportunity to be the primary carers of their children which many still appear to want to be. But free-market feminism is not just concerned to defend the free market against the strictures of anti-market feminists. It wants also to claim the market to be the most effective instrument available to women for removing whatever residual obstacles remain to their enjoying equality of opportunity. By allowing employers to pay unequal wages for the same work to men and women and to engage in reverse discrimination in favour of women as well as ordinary sexual discrimination against them, a free market would provide women with enormous opportunity to display their abilities if discriminated against by some employers, by offering their services at lower rates than men. It would also allow women to set up female-only businesses in which those women who would prefer such a working-environment could find space to explore their own potential, free from the pressure of men. It is likely that, in a free market, there would be a great plurality of different kinds of firm: some mixed, some male only, and some female only. Between them, these firms would employ a variety of different policies in relation to the sexual composition of their work force: some not practising any discrimination, others practising reverse discrimination in favour of one or other sex, and others old fashioned discrimination against one sex. However, I advocate the free market because the overall tendency in a freely competitive market would be that discrimination by any employer would be counter-productive and that selection and promotion would take place on the basis of merit. Otherwise, eventually, the discriminating firm would go out of business.

The suggestion has been that women have nothing to fear from such a degree of employment diversity being allowed, and much to gain. Among such gains, one is likely to be that many couples who would otherwise be unable but desirous of doing so will be able to get by on the income of only one full-time working partner, with the other devoting themselves full-time or part-time to the care of their children. There is no reason to think this is not something many women, and, for that matter, men, would not or should not be glad to have the opportunity to do.

The time has gone when, in order to prove themselves the equals of men, women need either deny their own special needs and differences from men, or demand from the state any special privileges and protection. Women who wish to enjoy the full spectrum of opportunities available to them today should favour the free market above all other possible instruments for availing them with these opportunities. Like so much else in the market, what use women choose to make of the opportunities it provides should be up to them. No one, not even well-intentioned feminists, has any right to tell men and women how they should organise their lives *vis-à-vis* one another. Nor should the law be used to dictate some form of organisation that corresponds with the personal wishes of only some. Women have not escaped—nor should they be encouraged to escape—the tyranny of men only to fall victim to a no less oppressive form of tyranny exercised by doctrinaire feminists. Bent upon imposing upon the majority of men and women their own personal and minority lifestyle preferences, the strident hostility towards the market character-istic of modern feminists is matched only by their ignorance of its workings and of its potential for advancing their wholly com-mendable cause of women's liberation and fulfilment.

With the collapse of communism, the time is long overdue for modern and post-modern feminists to re-appraise their typically hostile stance towards the market. Their doctrine was formed during a period when collectivist attitudes and economic dogmas had reached their apogee. Such attitudes and dogmas have been all but abandoned in the fields of enquiry from which they originally emanated. For those sympathetic to the general goal of feminism, it is time for them to reconsider their choice of path towards it. State socialism no longer holds the appeal it formerly had as a way of achieving the political ideals and objectives of its former supporters. Likewise, the market has come to be much more widely accepted as being better able than the state to organise and coordinate economic activity. So, too, it is to be expected that a candid and dispassionate re-examination of the anti-market measures advocated by modern feminism will reveal them to be similarly less suitable than the market for achieving the ultimate goal of feminism. It is in the hope of facilitating a critical re-examination of contemporary feminist orthodoxies that the present essay has been written.

Even Free Markets Need Feminism

Janet Radcliffe Richards

O NE of the best forms of political argument, if you can bring it off, is to show your opponents that *their own concerns*, properly understood, support not their own political conclusions, but yours. And this, essentially, is the aim of *Free-Market Feminism*. David Conway approves in general of free-market policies, but in this context his argument to free-market conclusions is addressed specifically to feminists. His claim is that many of the policies typically demanded and often achieved by feminists, such as anti-discrimination laws, affirmative action, equal pay for equal worth and state-provided childcare, work not only—like most other interventions in the freedom of the market—against the interests of society as a whole, but also against the interests of women. Feminists themselves should therefore be committed to free-market policies, and to opposing the familiar feminist interventions.

I want to argue that matters are really, at root, just the other way round. *Unless* there are positive interventions with specifically feminist aims, not only will there be little chance of righting what has been wrong about the position of women, but the economic achievements aimed at by free marketeers will themselves be lessened. The ideals underlying free-market economic strategies themselves support feminist intervention.

To argue that feminist policies of *some* kind are needed, on the other hand, is not to recommend any particular form of them. I agree with Conway that many of the policies he describes are ill-founded and carry serious disadvantages. The remedy for that, however, is not to abandon feminist policies altogether, but to interpret their purpose differently. When that is done, and the policies are adjusted to match, many of the problems do not arise.

To explain this it will be best not to address the contentious policies directly, but to but to go back to the beginnings of feminism and approach them from that direction.

The Beginnings of Feminism

When the modern feminist movement began to take off in the second half of the nineteenth century, the campaigners had two fundamental kinds of complaint about the position of women. One was about their subjection to men in marriage. Wives were legally in the power of their husbands, who also owned their property, their earnings, and, in effect, even their children. The other was about the exclusion of women from traditionally male territory. Women were excluded by laws and institutions from the franchise, political and public office, university education and the professions, and by general convention from most ways—certainly most adequately paid ways—of earning their own living. The early feminist campaign, therefore, was for legal and conventional equality: female suffrage on the same terms as male, equal access to education and employment, and an equal marriage contract.

As is well known, these aims were met for a long time with deeply entrenched and almost universal opposition. Feminist reform came slowly—voting on equal terms with men not until 1928—and was resisted at every stage by women as well as men. But what is particularly interesting, from the point of view of the present discussion, is that this resistance came against a background of widely accepted liberal ideals, both political and economic. The old idea of being born to a particular station in life had gradually been overtaken by the conviction—borne out by the increasing prosperity of the nations that practised it—that both individuals and society flourished if all positions and occupations were open to general competition, and people left free to rise by their own efforts. Samuel Smiles's *Self Help* (1859), with its improving tales of self-made men, was a secular bible of the late Victorian era.

This background put feminists in a strong intellectual position. Instead of having to argue for a whole new approach to politics, they were able to claim that *their opponents' own beliefs and principles* justified not the traditional position of women, as was claimed, but feminists' own demands. They, too, could engage in the useful strategy of invoking their opponents' professed principles in support of their own ends.

This kind of argument shows at its best in John Stuart Mill's *The Subjection of Women*,[1] which was published in 1869—two years after he had tried unsuccessfully, as a Member of Parliament, to have 'person' rather than 'man' written into the franchise-extending provisions of the 1867 Reform Act. This short book is a masterly piece of polemic, in which Mill tries to block every direction from which his traditionalist opponents might try to defend their position. And scattered throughout this range of arguments—not signalled as distinct—are several that take this particular form. Although in former times women's position—if it had been seriously challenged—would automatically have been defended in terms of religion, and although many of Mill's contemporaries did still argue in that way,[2] most of them were by that time trying to defend entrenched beliefs in terms of prevailing liberal values. And as Mill showed, these attempts to justify the old in terms of the new simply did not work. In one context after another, he demonstrated that his opponents' arguments depended on premises they themselves knew to be false or had no reason to believe true; or that their premises, even if true, did not support their political conclusions; or that the traditionalist conclusions they recommended were actually incompatible with principles they professed in other contexts. Or, quite often, all three at once.

For instance, one of the commonest arguments invoked to justify the exclusion of women from public life—familiar until very recently even in relatively enlightened parts of the world, and still muttered in corners—was that women should not undertake traditionally male activities because they were simply unsuited to them: women were incapable of doing men's work, and would only harm themselves and everyone else if they tried. On the surface, arguments like this sound as though they are rooted in the liberal idea that all people should do what suits them best, for their own good and the good of society; and because this principle sounds unexceptionable, most feminist critics have responded by denying the traditionalist claims about women's abilities. But this was not what Mill did. Instead of asserting contrary opinions of his own, he set about exposing a convoluted mass of confusions and inconsistencies within his opponents' beliefs and arguments.

In the first place, he pointed out, not even 'the most determined depreciator of women' could deny that at least some women had done everything that women were said to be unable to do, and had done well.[3] Second, since women's education and situation had systematically pushed them away from male activities (as everyone obviously knew, because that was the state of affairs traditionalists were trying to defend), nobody was in any position to attribute any lack of success to a lack of natural ability.[4] Third, if traditionalists really believed that women could not do these things, they should also believe that the existing selection criteria for any occupation—needed to keep out substandard men—would automatically exclude women,[5] and (although Mill did not put it quite like this) you cannot justify the existence of a rule by claiming that what it is designed to prevent would not happen anyway, without it. And finally, rules and conventions that confined women to their own sphere were incompatible with the liberal principles that by this time directed all other aspects of public policy, and which held that people should be free to achieve as much as they could, rather than being confined from birth to a particular role in life.

The clear implication of arguments like these was that the laws, institutions and conventions that kept women in their place were morally arbitrary. Their supporters tried to present them as compatible with, and even derived from, the general principles by which it was now widely agreed that society should be run; but this could not be done. The woman-suppressing and woman-excluding rules actually *overrode* the liberal principles from which they were supposed to be derived. And since, according to those ideas, society as a whole must be disadvantaged when work was not open to everyone who might want to compete for it, the exclusion of women not only deprived women themselves of access to many of the good things of life, but also resulted in the production of less for the good of all. Women were disadvantaged twice over, in being allocated an unfairly small share of an unfairly small whole. The woman-excluding rules achieved nothing but the arbitrary benefit of men at the expense of women.

Residues

Now it may be asked why all this is being laboured in a discussion of free-market feminism, since no present day free marketeer needs any persuading that rules excluding women are themselves inadmissible restrictions of market freedom. Free marketeers have no dispute with the nineteenth century form of feminism, in its pursuit of legal equality and the removal of obstacles to competition. They part company with other feminists only when moves are made to go beyond the ending of such formal obstacles, because, the argument goes, if you start making restrictive rules in the other direction, intervening in the free market on women's behalf, you just invert the original trouble. Special provisions for women, rather than competition on the same terms as men, lessen what can be produced for the good of all, as well as having counterproductive results for women themselves.[6]

In order to address the question of whether free marketeers are right to stop where they do, however, it is important to be clear about why they have come as far as this. Most free marketeers, and certainly David Conway, do not recommend the freedom of markets as a self-standing principle, to be adopted irrespective of its consequences. Unlike political libertarianism, which tends to be rooted in the idea that people simply have a right to be as free as possible of government interference, free-market economics is usually based on the *empirical* belief that a free market offers the most effective mechanism for producing what is best for society as whole. No free marketeer, furthermore, believes that this will come about through a complete absence of government intervention, and a return to some hypothetical state of nature; free markets cannot possibly function well without a framework of laws and regulations. The free-market objection to the formal exclusion of women, therefore, must be understood as based on the empirical belief that this will result in a lower total product for the good of all. But if this is the problem, can the mere removal of formal restrictions be expected to put matters to rights? What has to be considered is not the case of some imaginary community starting from scratch, but of a society with an uninterrupted history of women's exclusion from the male sphere; and it seems overwhelmingly likely that even when the woman-excluding rules are abolished, they will leave behind residues that continue their work by less formal means, and still place systematic obstacles in the way of women's fulfilling their potential.

In the first place, it is significant that arguments like those of Mill—cast iron in their logic, and to us seeming unanswerable—made virtually no impression on his contemporaries. It seemed to them so obviously right that women should occupy their traditional sphere that no amount of reasoning and evidence could dent their conviction—as Mill himself was well aware.[7] If people simply could not see the logical and empirical absurdities to which they were driven in their attempts to justify the sexes' separate spheres, even when these were demonstrated with total lucidity, how likely is it that the removal of formal restrictions would result in employers' suddenly starting to assess women candidates and employees on exactly the same terms as men? It seems much more likely that the habitual rationalising would simply shift to a different level, and manifest itself in the form of particular excuses for not appointing particular women to particular positions. ('Of course her paper qualifications were good, but she somehow just didn't seem to have the right kind of approach to the work...')

It is difficult to prove directly that this sort of thing goes on (and just as difficult to prove that it does not)—especially as a good deal of it is likely to be unconscious. But as well as the reasonable presumption that it is almost bound to happen, systematic experiments have borne out the suspicion. Experiments some years ago, for instance, showed that if names were changed on student essays or academic articles, to make it look as though they were written by an author of the other sex, that radically altered the assessment of the work;[8] a female name significantly lowered the perception of its quality. And this kind of informal discrimination against women has just the same effect as the formal kind, in allowing less good men to be employed in preference to better women.

Second, such deeply ingrained attitudes will affect not merely the *perception* of women's work, but also, in many situations, the quality itself. It is well established, for instance, that expectations have a strong influence on performance, and if people look at women with the expectation of their doing less well than men, that is what will often come about. Positive obstacles to success are also likely to lie in the attitudes of hostile colleagues and sceptical clients. No matter how competent a woman may be in her understanding of motor mechanics, and no matter how well her employer understands her abilities, a presumption by her potential customers that women can know nothing useful about cars will make her less successful in selling them than would be an intrinsically less knowledgeable, but more publicly plausible, man.

Third, there is the obvious fact that working patterns developed while women occupied only the lowest levels of the workforce. This is bound to be significant. Most obviously, arrangements are likely to be much less compatible with active child rearing than they might have been if women had been involved from the beginning; and this in turn probably means that women who want look after their own children are less productive in other ways than need have been the case.[9] Another kind of difficulty may lie in established methods of work, and procedures for assessing the potential competence of employees. If women tend to have different ways of working from men (which may well be true, though as yet we have inadequate evidence either way), they may not perform as well in male-created environments as they otherwise might. And unfamiliar female approaches to established tasks, even if potentially effective, may seem like incompetence when measured by standards developed for the assessment of a different style of work, and lead by yet another route to the underemployment of women.

Finally, the combination of all these actuals and possibles means that adequate evidence of women's potential is simply unavailable, and that what evidence there is—of women's not working at all in some areas, and doing less well than men in others—may well misrepresent their real potential even to the most impartial investigator. Until women have had the chance to do what they were, for a long time, not allowed to do, they will not be able to provide evidence that they can do it.

None of this has anything to do with 'under-representation' of women in any position. It depends on no claim at all about whether women are or are not as good as (or better than) men at anything or everything, or how many women ought to occupy particular positions, or whether women really do do things differently from men. The claim is only that there are strong reasons to think that positive impediments to women's contributing their best to the general good will outlast the disappearance of merely formal obstacles; and that *if* women's abilities are being under-used in this way, that should be of as much concern to non-dogmatic free marketeers as to feminists. As before the removal of formal restrictions on women, the concerns of free marketeers and feminists still coincide.

Self Rectification

There is, however, an obvious free-market response to this: that even if all this is true, the free market itself provides the best remedy for whatever problems remain. Let things take their own course, it will be said, unimpeded by central interference, and the market will weed out these residues of women's traditional exclusion. Some employers will spot women of high potential and employ them, and their businesses will flourish in consequence; others who persist in preferring less good men will gradually sink. Employers who are ingenious enough to devise ways of making women's work more compatible with child rearing, or better adapted to women's ways of working, will become increasingly successful, while the ones who are resistant to change will wither away as they should.

But how plausible is this idea? Given the foregoing account of what the problems are, there are several reasons for doubting that a free market can be relied on to work in this way.[10]

First, although in a free market the enterprises that survive must be in some sense the best, the only thing they are necessarily best at is survival itself—and in those particular circumstances. The question of whether they will also be best from *any other* point of view, and how reliably so, is different and empirical. A free market will indeed weed out hopelessly bad products, but it notoriously cannot be relied on to make sure that the best are the ones that survive; if the producer of the second best has more commercial clout or acumen than the producer of the best, the best may struggle or disappear.[11] The same applies to the enlightened spotters of women's potential. If businesses were equal in other respects, and large numbers of employers took on valuable women while others systematically excluded them, women's employment might make the difference between what survived and what did not; but in real situations a willingness and ability to make full use of women is only one variable among many. It might make no systematic difference to what kinds of enterprise flourished.

Second, whether you do well in a competition depends not on your doing *as well as possible*, but only on how you compare with your competitors. People are notoriously unreliable maximisers of what economists would regard as their own interests, and if everybody else is as ineffectual in this way as you are, there is nothing the market on its own can do to eliminate any of you. If everyone is full of the preconceptions and prejudices that obstruct the full use of women's potential, you will be at no competitive disadvantage with your own. And just in case anyone argues that this is most unlikely, and that someone is bound to make the breakthrough that leads to competitive advantage, the history of women's emancipation itself shows just how easily stagnation can happen. Even in the nineteenth century there were no laws against employing women in the higher levels of industry and commerce, but there was no sign of enlightened employers' putting women into senior positions and flourishing as a result; most industrialists and professionals were like everyone else, in not even taking seriously the possibility that women might occupy these positions and in automatically resisting change. It was feminist pressure, and later the necessities of two world wars, rather than the market, that slowly brought about improvement.

Third, there is also a quite different kind of problem, well known to economists, about the connection between individually beneficial choices and what is generally good. Even if people could be relied on to maximise their individual interests in the way the market hopes, there are many contexts in which this can offer no possible—let alone certain—route to the best general outcome.[12] There are limits to the effectiveness of Adam Smith's invisible hand. Suppose, for instance, you are astute enough to see through the cultural clutter to the abilities of the woman motor mechanic, but know that the prejudiced public will make her less effective in her work of car-selling than an intrinsically inferior man would be. Free-market rationality dictates your going for the inferior man. It would be best for everyone (except the less good men) if the prejudice could end so that such women could make full use of their potential, but that is unlikely to happen until people are used to car saleswomen, and the market cannot provide any reliable route to such a situation. The same may be true of potentially valuable attempts to reorganise working practices. You may, perhaps, calculate that special concessions and subsidies to child-rearing employees would be more than paid for by those women's later performance when they returned to full-time work; but if you were to implement these arrangements unilaterally, you would (in a free market) run the risk that, after you had made the concessions, some other employer would come in and pick up the reward. The market, therefore, makes sure that no individual provides such concessions.

Perhaps the free-market reply to this may be that in the long run all such matters are bound to put themselves to rights. But even if this were certain—and when possible mechanisms are considered in detail, it is hard to see how it could be—the long run is not good enough. In the long run the earth will be swallowed up by the sun. If making the best use of women's potential matters, it matters to do this as soon as possible, for the benefit of as many people as possible.

The freedom of markets is not an all-or-nothing matter, but one of degree. Anyone whose general inclination towards free markets is not dogmatic, but stems from an empirical belief that the best way to produce what is generally good for society lies in this direction rather than in state-controlled economies, must recognise that there may be ways in which centrally organised nudges can improve the direction a generally free market takes. If these arguments have been right, the situation of women is a case in point. Since there are many reasons for believing that the market on its own cannot reliably undo the effects of the long subjection of women, it seems that direct feminist action, of a co-ordinated and central kind, will be needed to end the situation of women's having an unfairly small share of the unfairly small whole. And the small whole should be of as much concern to the non-dogmatic free marketeer as the small share is to feminists.

Possible Remedies

How, then, should a feminist of free-market inclinations proceed? Other kinds of feminist, whose political theories prescribe particular outcomes—equal numbers of men and women in important positions, perhaps, or free, state-provided childcare—as essential *in themselves*, have in some ways a relatively easy task; they have only to campaign politically for the achievement of already clear aims. But feminists who approach from the other direction—wanting to remove certain kinds of obstruction, but not to specify in advance what should result from this—have particularly difficult problems, because once the formal restrictions have been removed it becomes increasingly unclear what to count as obstacles. Free-market and other liberal feminists have good reason to believe that shadows of the past are still falling over the present and impeding the full use of women's abilities, and that these are not likely to be eliminated without special, concerted effort; but they still have to determine what form that effort should take, and how to judge whether the results are going in the right direction.

As a first move, it seems reasonable to recognise the problems identified here as being of two broad kinds. First, there are likely to be deep residual preconceptions about the place and abilities of women, which distort individual judgments about women's potential, make their work actually less good than it should be, and make it difficult even for the open-minded and unprejudiced to get adequate evidence about women's potential. And second, nearly all aspects of economic organisation developed in a male-dominated environment, without any consideration of the possibility that women might tend to work better in systematically different ways, and flourish in different circumstances. When the matter is put like that, two directions of activity, corresponding to the two problems, suggest themselves.

First, the most obvious way to counteract ingrained habits of mind in our naturally conservative species is to try to get ourselves used to other possibilities. If everyone became familiar with seeing women and men in each other's situations, that might start to loosen the preconceptions, and open the way to more objective judgments. What kinds of measure might seem plausible to someone who wanted to bring this about? One obvious possibility would be anti-discrimination legislation, partly to make sure that women were put into previously male areas whenever they were objectively well suited to the positions in question, but also to keep everyone aware of the need to try to make impartial assessments, and to strengthen the hands of those who had to contend with obstructive colleagues. Another possibility would be to adopt affirmative action policies of various sorts, to put more women into men's areas, and vice versa, than would otherwise happen. And, since low status and low perceptions of ability are often strongly correlated with low levels of pay, yet another possibility would be to insist on increases in women's pay, especially in area of work where it seemed plausible to attribute the existing rates not to the pressures of the market, but to a deep presumption that women's work must be less valuable than men's.[13]

Second, when there are ways of reorganising work that look as though they might allow women to be more productive, but which no one has any incentive to institute individually because of the costs and risks involved, or because some experiment could not possibly work unless a large number of organisations tried it at once, the state should act as the agency for *sharing out* those risks and costs by means of subsidies from tax revenues, and as the co-ordinator of larger scale experiments. And in this context, one of the most important areas for consideration would be making the fullest use of women with children.

There does, in other words, seem to be a *prima facie* case for state intervention, and along lines similar to those of familiar feminist policies.

Replies to Objections

Nevertheless, the case is so far only *prima facie*. If policies such as these are recommended not as morally required in their own right, but as a means to eliminating unwelcome residues of the past, the presumption in their favour may be overridden by stronger considerations against them. I have tried to show so far that the free market cannot on its own be relied on to remove the continuing effects of women's formal exclusion from male territory; but if there are strong enough objections to feminist interventions of these kinds, perhaps a free market may yet, in spite of its inadequacies, be the best option available for feminists and everyone else. What, then, can be said about the objections raised by free-market critics to feminist policies such as these?

There is no space for details, but the broad answer is this. If feminist policies of the familiar kind are recommended on the basis of the kinds of argument offered here, those policies should automatically take a form to which most of these objections do not even arise.

When participants in a movement like feminism are formulating their political policies, it matters crucially that they should work out not only what their policies should be, but what their *justification* is. People often have radically different reasons for their united support of some particular end (the European Community might be resisted by the combined forces of fox-hunting Little Englanders and animal rights campaigners against live exports), which is why you can often get ideological opponents to support your policies by means of appealing to their own concerns. But the *reasons* you have for adopting any policy will determine your attitude to its form and extent, and if people differ in their reasons for recommending some broad policy, they will soon find themselves disagreeing about details. The reason any feminist has for looking favourably on policies like affirmative action or state provision of childcare will critically determine the form she thinks they should take; and the obstacle-removing arguments for state intervention that might be considered by a free-market feminist have quite different implications for details of policy from other feminist arguments that are rooted in ideas of women's intrinsic entitlement to certain benefits.

Suppose, for instance, you are inclined to support feminist policies of the anti-discrimination, affirmative action, equal pay kind. What is your reason? Many feminists, probably most, regard anti-discrimination legislation as necessary because they think it intrinsically unjust to allow sex, or (a different matter) sex-connected characteristics, to be taken into consideration in the making of appointments. Many feminists support affirmative action because they think it intrinsically right to have equal numbers of men and women in most areas, or (again a different matter) to compensate women for past discrimination. They may also demand equal pay for equal worth because they think it inherently right that pay should be proportional to some kind of worth. For reasons obviously beyond the scope of this paper, I think all these lines of argument are mistaken. But, mistaken or not, they are certainly *different* from the prejudice-dislodging justifications for such policies that have so far been suggested here. And the difference is crucial, because if your reasons for supporting feminist policies are of this second kind, that will automatically drive them into a form that leaves them no longer open to most of the familiar objections.

Consider, for instance the usual lines of objection to affirmative action policies. It is often said that if we appoint inadequate women to previously male-dominated areas, that will only confirm and entrench existing prejudices about the unsuitability of women. It is also said that such practices are unjust to men, since women will be given the jobs that the men are entitled to. But if affirmative action policies are set up *specifically for the purpose* of dislodging prejudice, they will automatically take a form that avoids these objections. Since it would be essential not to risk appointments that could confirm prejudices, affirmative action policies that were justified in this way would have to be limited to such things as active recruitment and giving preference to women when other things were equal, and to reverse discrimination only to the extent that any lowering of standards for women was publicly imperceptible. This would also avoid the objection that women were being given jobs to which men were entitled, even if such entitlements are thought to exist. If the past can be presumed to have left a residue of obstacles to women's success, it must also be presumed that men are still getting jobs to which women are, by those criteria, really entitled; and in that case a marginal discrimination in favour of women would be unlikely to do more than restore the balance, if indeed that much.[14]

Much the same applies to the matter of anti-discrimination laws. Most people probably do accept that these are justified because people with certain characteristics have an intrinsic entitlement to particular jobs; but even if Conway is right to dispute this (and I agree with him, though I am not sure how he squares this with the idea that reverse discrimination is unfair to the men who ought to be given the jobs that go to women), anti-discrimination laws instituted *for the reasons suggested here* are not open to this objection. The underlying idea, once again, is only a proposed strategy for undoing what look like the worst effects of the past, and, as such, not intended as permanent. Whatever we think about the acceptability in the long run of allowing people to act on simple preferences for one sex over the other as employees or associates—and I think the matter is far more complicated than it is usually taken to be—there is good reason *now* to insist on the breaking down of male-only bastions, because until recently male terrain has encompassed nearly all positions of power and influence, as well as most areas of higher human endeavour. That must be got out of the system before we can start to work out whether an ideal arrangement would allow for a certain amount of simple preference on grounds of sex; and if women had to wait until men felt inclined to let them in, experience suggests they would have a long wait. For now we must insist on the full integration of women, just to get the barriers down.

A similar reply could also be made to objections to policies to increase women's pay. There are indeed all kinds of absurdities in the idea that there can be an objective assessment of the worth of incommensurable kinds of work, quite apart from any objections (from the political left) that everyone is of equal worth, or (from the right) that the only reasonable measure of worth is what is successful in the market. But insistence on increasing women's pay in some areas, where it seemed likely to counteract traditional assumptions about women's natural inferiority, would not be open to any of these objections.

And, finally, a similar case might even be made for state organising and financing of childcare—though this is probably the most complicated issue of all. Once again, much turns on the reasons underlying whatever is proposed.

My own view is that the idea of free, state-supplied childcare as a permanent solution to the problems of working parents is, for all kinds of reasons, many of them feminist, *nothing like radical enough*.[15] It leaves the basic structures of work—the ones that developed when women were excluded—untouched, and as unsuited as ever to the needs of women (or men) who want to care personally for their children and to make the fullest possible use of their other abilities as well. The issue here is a fundamental matter of social organisation that we have hardly begun to think about seriously enough: the double problem of how to arrange family responsibilities between men and women, and of how to reconcile the structures of work with the demands of family life. How all this can best be achieved is still anyone's guess.

One reasonable guess, however, is that the best ways are most likely to be found by enterprising and inventive women who are in a position to set up organisations with this problem specifically in mind. For this to happen, they need the kind of experience that will give them enough understanding of the working world to recognise feasible possibilities, and enough economic and political power to give their projects a flying start. (Once again, the mere quality of a project is not enough to ensure its survival.) We cannot force innovative ideas to appear, but we can try to make sure women are in a strong position to start the innovating by giving state support—perhaps including readily available childcare—to projects that will allow this to happen. And since *this* reason for suggesting such possibilities has nothing to do with claims that women have a natural right to decide to have children while everyone else pays for them, or that women should be discouraged from looking after their own children, it is not open to objections of those kinds. Yet again, such measures could be seen as temporary, and among many other efforts to give better possibilities a chance to emerge.

And to move beyond the specific issue of childcare to that of the restructuring of work in general, it is worth mentioning that the general approach being recommended here also meets many of the familiar objections to state interventions of other kinds. To the extent that the state's purpose is to act as a sharer-out of risk in experiments whose success would benefit everybody, or as a co-ordinator and controller of collective policies in contexts where individual choices cannot produce the right cumulative effects, it is acting not as a nanny state, against individual freedom, nor as a centralised organiser of industry and commerce. If it acts for these reasons it does only what free individuals would prefer, but are unable to bring about through unilateral action.

Conclusion: A Wider Context

The overall conclusion is that even if you accept the ideas of free-market economics—a matter left wide open here—you should still, on your own principles, be in favour of specifically feminist government policies. It is not plausible to take the view that once the specifically feminist project of removing the restrictions on women has succeeded everything else can be left to the market, and that the free-market feminist is one whose feminist work is essentially over. There is overwhelming reason to think both that the effects of women's long exclusion from the market will remain after the formal constraints have gone, and that the market itself is most unlikely to be a reliable rectifier of this problem. The free marketeer's own concern that women should play as full a part as possible in the market, for their own good and everyone else's, should therefore be seen as supporting the conclusion that specifically feminist interventions are still needed, and even that some of the most appropriate may take forms resembling those of familiar feminist policies. If they are considered in the light of the justification offered here, that will automatically modify the details in such a way as to obviate many of the criticisms a free marketeer would make of similar policies in their more familiar forms, and with their standard feminist justifications.

However, the conclusion is really wider than this. It is not just that free marketeers should, on their own principles, support feminist interventions of these kinds. It is that *everybody* should support them on their own principles, whatever their general political ideals. The reason is that the fundamental feminist complaint, as identified here, is that women were traditionally subjected to men and excluded from the male sphere not *because of* prevailing political attitudes, but *in spite of* them. The subjection of women worked as an *overrider* of values that were otherwise accepted. And this was not simply, if at all, a matter of cynical calculation by men with vested interests; the convictions about a woman's place were so deep that they were believed in their own right, and automatically rationalised—with fudges and inventions of every kind to cover the gaps—in terms of publicly acceptable principles, and by women as well as men. And since this is the case, it must be presumed that traditional attitudes to women, unless tackled in their own right, are likely to act as overriders of *any* general principles that anyone hopes to implement: communist, socialist, social democrat, moderate liberal, or libertarian. Furthermore, this is not just a theoretical possibility. We have already seen how the subjection of women survived the massive change of political principle from traditional Toryism to liberalism in nineteenth-century Britain; and it survived in much the same way the radical upheavals of the French, American and Russian revolutions, with all their reforming zeal.

This means, in principle, that everyone should be willing to unite in the kind of feminism I have been describing—the kind that is bent on removing the residues of women's arbitrary disadvantage—as a lowest common denominator of what needs to be done. Beyond that point there will inevitably appear substantive disagreements, but until then, there can be a considerable unanimity of purpose, shared by everybody except dyed-in-grain conservatives, and, of course, those men who want to hold on to their large share of a small whole.

This is not an easy kind of feminism to embrace. It is not easy to have as an objective the removal of obstacles whose nature is so elusive, and to work at problems for whose solution there is no clear criterion of success. However, similar problems arise in most areas of politics. We often think there is no single right solution to some problem, but nevertheless are sure that matters could be better, and try to push them in promising directions. What we know of the past gives us strong reason to believe that present-day arrangements are unlikely to allow the best possible use of women's potential. This needs to be addressed as a problem in its own right. The fact that we shall not know when we have reached the best answer is not a good reason for pursuing instead aims that are clear but wrong, any more than the elusiveness of the problem is a reason for denying that it still exists. Feminism is not yet at an end for any kind of feminist, free-market or otherwise.

Feminist Goals in a
Free-Market Society

Brenda Almond

B EHIND the concerns expressed in David Conway's essay lies
a genuine feminist dilemma. The nature of the dilemma was
highlighted at the beginning of the 1990s, following the changes
in Eastern Europe, when the former communist countries threw
off the yoke of centralised economic control, and prepared to
draw deep breaths of the heady air of market freedom. Not least
of the expectations current at the time were those of a small
number of women in Eastern European countries who, with
minimal attention or publicity, supported nascent and low-profile
feminist movements in their own locality. Their expectations,
however, may well have been coloured by the picture of the
lifestyle of women in Western countries projected by Hollywood
and by internationally-marketed TV soap-operas. It would have
been natural for anyone with only a second-hand acquaintance
with life in the USA, for example, to assume that what capitalist
plenty brought for women was freedom from the burden of
combining domestic and family life with a full-time 'real' job in
the outside world. Indeed, as a spectator on the sidelines at the
time, I sensed a moment of confusion as feminists of the Eastern
Bloc met feminists from the West, and found to their surprise
that they were confronting a very different political agenda, and
different preoccupations.

As they quickly discovered, the freedoms sought by Western
feminists were precisely those already 'enjoyed' under communism: freedom to work outside the home on equal terms with
men; ready access to abortion as a means of family limitation;
and access to state-provided childcare facilities from the child's
earliest months—arrangements designed to meet parents' needs
to cover for long adult working-days rather than children's needs
for a little early social and educational stimulus outside the

home. And behind all this, for couples or families in the Eastern Bloc countries where such arrangements were routine, lay the hard reality of the economic impossibility of living on a single adult wage.

The ensuing attempt to forge a common agenda from the diverse aspirations of women's groups under different economic regimes has highlighted a central paradox in what women want. In part the agenda of Western feminists is explained by the fact that, in the liberal democracies, those in a position to define what women want are overwhelmingly women in academic or journalistic occupations which allow them to control their time, their working-hours and their energies—or else women in a committed relationship with men who are able and willing to resolve their domestic problems because they themselves are in occupations of this sort. And the solutions such activists seek are more likely, where very young children are concerned, to involve employing a substitute carer in the home than making use of a 10-hour daily creche. For others—the majority—the choice is starker, since it has be be based on accepting the inevitability of the absence of both parents from the home for the whole of the working day and the financial impracticability of providing a substitute in the home. The feminist movement in both the USA and Europe did a disservice to working-class women in failing to appreciate this fact or to register its implications.

Instead, rather than focussing on these fundamental if rather mundane and prosaic matters, Western feminism has defined itself, as Conway points out, by division into schools of thought on a more theoretical basis. One broadly accepted taxonomy of feminist positions involves a fourfold classification: conservative feminists who are concerned to protect the interests of women who stay at home in the 'traditional' role; liberal feminists who want to open up opportunities for women to play an equal role with men in the world outside the home by removing any political or legal obstacles in their way; socialist feminists anxious to do this through the transfer of domestic and family responsibilities to the state; and separatist feminists, often lesbian separatists, concerned to develop a wholly independent mode of female existence.[1] The more recent emergence of a post-modern feminism rooted in the ideas of philosophers such as Jacques Derrida, Michel Foucault and, in the USA, Richard Rorty, reproduces elements of the last two of these, but repudiates the attempt to provide a universal analysis of women's needs across differences in culture, class and ethnicity.[2]

Nevertheless, the contemporary feminist movement is beginning to recognise that, if it is to play a role on the world stage, it must define itself internationally in more general terms. One way of doing this is to define feminism very simply as a movement for improving the lot and position of women of all social classes under all political regimes. It is worth noting, however, that feminists promoting this ideal do not necessarily extend the idea of a common cause or common goals to cover cultural or religious variation, and may be unwilling to condemn policies such as sex-selective abortion and infanticide, female circumcision, arranged or forced marriages, for fear of violating some principle of cultural autonomy. The philosophical influence of post-modernism tends to reinforce this tendency to cultural and moral relativism, and its application to practical issues, even where there is no overt or conscious commitment to the theory.

It may be more difficult than it looks, then, to achieve consensus on aims and aspirations, and, even where apparent agreement on aims *is* achieved, the same divisions may resurface as disagreement about methods and strategies. So, while it is unlikely that anyone would disagree with the broad aim of improving the lot of women, the Western influence, which is extremely strong in the international feminist movement, has been to perceive this goal as attainable by freeing women from economic dependence on individual men—something to be achieved by the twin strategies of a) transferring this dependency from the individual to the state and b) introducing legally enforceable anti-discrimination policies. Since these two strategies raise very different considerations, it will be useful to separate discussion of them here.

Transferring Dependency

It is tempting to seek to fulfil women's aspirations to autonomy by substituting dependence on the state—the body of taxpayers—for dependence on husband or partner, where women cannot easily be financially independent themselves, e.g. when caring for very young children. Bertrand Russell was one of the first to note that this might have broader political implications when he wrote, in 1929 in *Marriage and Morals*, that:

If the State were to adopt the role of the father, the State would, *ipso facto*, become the sole capitalist. Thoroughgoing Communists have often maintained the converse, that if the State is to be the sole capitalist, the family, as we have known it, cannot survive.[3]

What Russell might have added is that transfer of responsibility for the family from the individual to the state does not in fact make women *independent*—it merely makes their dependency more diffuse. As far as transfer of responsibility is concerned, then, recourse to the taxpayer only obscures the real issues, for the inevitable and natural stage of dependency around childbirth and early child-raising—inevitable at least under modern conditions— is something which affects all but a small minority of women who are wealthy through inheritance or through their own earning capacity.

Nevertheless, contemporary political communities of all types have set in train the transfer of ultimate responsibility for this phase of female dependency from the individual to the state, either for ideological reasons or from motives of compassion for individual women and their children caught in situations not of their own choosing. It is now being generally recognised, however, that this policy has had a number of adverse social effects and indeed that it has produced social trends absolutely opposed to female welfare.[4] These include the breakdown of families on a scale that was never foreseen, particularly when combined with the creation, through over-flexible and accommodating divorce laws, of insecurity in a central relationship that needs to be rock-solid if it is to provide a viable base for a project—the raising of children—which may take twenty years or more. It is worth asking why it is that Britain leads the Western European nations in the incidence of divorce and in numbers of one-parent families.[5] Clearly the answer can only be that, as far as the first of these is concerned, while under free-market conditions it is exceptional for a man to be able to support two families, generous and indiscriminate welfare provision makes this 'privilege' of the rich accessible to everyone. As far as the second is concerned, again under free-market conditions, saving and sacrifice on the part of a couple is essential to provide, first of all, a roof and then reliable financial support throughout the process of child-bearing and child-raising. This 'market' aspect is nullified by routine mandatory provision of accommodation and support for single parents.

There is, then, a reciprocal relationship between the strength or weakness of families and the state's detachment from or involvement in private life. But this is not to imply that the state has no role in protecting the interests of the vulnerable. On the contrary, even without a deliberate policy of transferring dependency, state involvement will very often expand to fill the vacuum left by individuals, for genuine dependency must be covered one way or another in a modern society, as reaction to the presence of homeless mentally or physically ill people on the streets of major cities shows. And while the libertarian does indeed favour minimal state involvement, this does not necessarily exclude action to protect vulnerable categories of people, for the basic philosophy of the social contract theorists who stand as the founders of Western democratic liberalism included the protection of the weak as part of its programme from the start. There can be no doubt that all individuals come into this category of vulnerability in their early years, and, while Hobbes (1588-1679) and Locke (1632-1704) would not have separated children's interests from those of their father, today, legally and morally, their separate status *is* recognised. Recognising this obligation, however, does not necessarily entail making direct cash payments to a carer; and indeed, the social experience of recent decades would suggest that the most effective way to protect the interests of children is for the state to uphold the contract entered into by their parents, whether formally or informally. While 'family' has recently become a politically contentious concept, it is worth recalling that the idea of 'family' is rooted in the older and simpler idea of household, and that the function of families is to meet a range of practical needs: common residence, economic co-operation, sexual relationships, reproduction, raising children. Most of these functions depend upon secure arrangements, the failure of which impacts upon the vulnerable—both considerations germane to a liberal philosophy in its classical form. It is this failure to recognise that even a libertarian 'minimal state' is politically committed to preserving contracts and protecting the weak from actual harm by stronger parties that creates an apparent fissure on the right of politics between political conservatives and libertarians; at the same time, it shows that such a gulf is unnecessary if the basic principles of classical liberalism common to both are understood.

If it is relevant to consider the origins and evolution of ideas in the case of the transfer of dependency argument, it may be helpful to do the same when considering the second strategy that is at issue—protective legislation in the labour market. The origins of this essentially egalitarian claim are closely intertwined with the origins and evolution of a feminist movement.

The Historical Background

Since militant feminism is often depicted as a force which has appeared only in the last two decades, and then mainly to be a thorn in the flesh of the conservative right, it is worth recalling that it is, as an ideology and a movement, very much older than this. Women's equality with men in capacities and potential was recognised by Plato in the fifth century BC and, significantly, Plato also recognised that, if this potential were to be released, there might be drastic implications for the restructuring of society. In particular, Plato considered that female equality was incompatible with individual family life and indeed with individual homes and possessions. It is true, however, that Plato's ideas remained in the realm of philosophical fantasy until the modern period. Straws in the wind indicative of new thinking on women's capacities at the beginning of this period are to be found, however, in such negative indications of climate of opinion as Molière's play *Les Femmes Savantes (Clever Women)* (1672) which attests in its mockery of them to the existence of a class of educated women engaged in political or literary debate in seventeenth-century France. Not so long afterwards, too, a class of women existed, in England as well as France, who were capable of being incensed by Rousseau's well-known but sorry proposals for female education in his *Émile* (1762).[6]

But the modern era of reflection on these issues really begins with Mary Wollstonecraft (1759-97),[7] followed by a succession of liberal thinkers, not least of whom was John Stuart Mill (1806-73), author of the classic defence of individual liberty and advocate of women's liberation, who was writing in England at around the same time as a movement for female advance and emancipation was gaining impetus in the USA. Mill's example shows quite clearly that, in its classical liberal form, the cause of female emancipation is fully compatible with an individualist and libertarian position. Nevertheless, Mill's endorsement of this cause was still muted by comparison with the more radical conclusions of Harriet Taylor. The difference between them is summed up by Alice Rossi in this way:

> Harriet took the more radical position: if women are not to barter their persons for bread, they not only must be well educated but must be permitted to enter any occupational field they wish. Mill took the more cautious position, that a woman's goal would continue to be marriage to a man she loved; her occupation after marriage would be to 'adorn and beautify life' by sharing fully and intelligently her husband's occupations and interests ... Mill saw no benefit to a wife's contributing to the income of the family, on the grounds that her work in the household and the rearing of children were her contribution to the family unit.[8]

Many people in the late nineteenth and early twentieth centuries, including female activists themselves, shared Mill's more limited goals and believed that the battle would be over when women won the vote. It is an irony, then, that this goal was ultimately achieved, not through the winning of the moral argument, but rather because of the need to use women's labour and capacities to maintain the home front during the two world wars while men were otherwise engaged. Once suffrage was won, and the feminist movement did proceed to campaign on workplace issues, the approach was still liberal or libertarian in the sense that it took it for granted that legal and political equality to provide a framework for choice were all that was required to render the position of women acceptable. While there is certainly a question as to whether it is desirable to try to go beyond this, it is hard to see any case for seeking a return to the situation that prevailed earlier when women did not have parity of legal rights in respect of children, property, inheritance, etc. What, then, is the objection of Conway to a more extensive legal equality? Could it be an objection to something that could be described as the *spoonfeeding* of liberty?

Anti-discrimination Laws

The question, then, is whether anti-discrimination laws and equal opportunity legislation do in fact spoonfeed liberty. Are they an attempt to cosset a newly-privileged class? The libertarian case *for* anti-discrimination legislation can be put like this: liberals (classical liberals, or libertarians) have historically been opposed to patronage and preferment, and the issue here—privilege by reason of birth—is just as objectionable if it is sex-based as if it is based on the more ancient and traditional preferments of social caste, connection and class. There is, then, a *prima facie* case for liberals to support women's rights. Of course, for a huge and expanding anti-discrimination *industry* to grow up at the expense of the taxpayer is a disaster. But there is nothing wrong with laws that make it unambiguously clear that the complacent and open operation of prejudice is illegal—nothing wrong, that is, from a *libertarian* point of view, for —to repeat—the libertarian concedes the need for laws which protect the individual from harm by other stronger parties, and the harm of being prevented from earning a living is certainly as serious as physical attack and injury. But if there are laws, some effort must be made to enforce them. The ethical or ideological point is that the root of the liberal position is its concern for individual freedom. That freedom can indeed be breached if someone finds herself consistently unable to work, or repeatedly passed over in appointments in favour of inferior rivals, on no other basis than a set of assumptions made because those rivals are male. This is the problem of what Mill called 'ascribed statuses'. Rossi quotes Mill's remarks on this:

> The principle of the modern movement in morals and politics is that conduct and conduct alone entitles to respect: that not what men are but what they do constitutes their claim to deference ... human beings are no longer born to their place in life ... individual choice is our model now.[9]

She adds:

> To the generations of the twentieth century who have seen tyranny and the suppression of human liberty in all forms of government—Fascist, Communist, and democratic—John Stuart Mill's invocation of the rights of men and women to liberty and justice have a strong, continuing appeal.[10]

It would be absurd and wrong, then, in my opinion, to abandon such principles. If we look for the true source of the complaints of people who share Conway's doubts, we find that these doubts centre, not on the theoretical position, but on what happens in practice. Advocates of equal treatment too easily assume that the claimants *are* offering an equal contribution to the workplace or the role, and this is, for excellent and obvious reasons, very often not the case. It is necessary, then, to distinguish the claim that what a person is offering is as good as what someone else is offering from the very different claim that, while it is admitted to be of lesser value, the person concerned is not to be blamed for that fact and still needs to be allowed to work. This, after all, was what produced legislation following the two world wars compelling employers to take on a percentage of disabled men. There was no pretence that a man who had lost a leg fighting for his country could provide as efficient service in many occupations as an able-bodied man, but in that particular case there was a strong public will not to leave men who had made such sacrifices for their country on the scrap-heap of unemployment.

To repeat, then, although the principle is sound, its application is a problem. Women with family responsibilities are very often *not* in as strong a position as the unattached. They will often prefer less money for less responsibility, less work-place stress, shorter hours, the ability to be absent at short notice or no notice at all. Men, too, sometimes find themselves in situations in which they would be willing to make a trade-off in these terms. A sick wife, elderly parents, partner desertion or death, or personal psychological or physical difficulties are all situations in which a rigid eight a.m to six p.m. absence from the house five days a week may be just as much of a problem for a man to cope with, as is the typical 'woman's' problem of caring for young children. It should be possible for people of either sex to opt for employment negotiated with such needs acknowledged, at whatever reduced rate of pay their employer will consider fair compensation for engaging an employee whose contribution to the enterprise is likely to be handicapped by personal factors. But it should also be possible for women prepared to offer genuinely equal work to be guaranteed equal treatment, i.e. women who are prepared to regard it as their *own*, not their employer's problem, that households depend on shopping and cooking being accomplished, and that sick children need to stay home from school; that the school day is shorter than the typical working-day, and so on. Critics are right to say, however, that what is *not* reasonable is to ask for special consideration *and* equal pay. This even applies to the issue—often regarded as sacrosanct—of maternity leave: it is unreasonable to deny that a prolonged absence at an unplanned time can leave an organisation in disarray, and unreasonable, therefore, not to acknowledge that there is a cost to be attached to this.

Conclusions

The practical measures objected to by Conway are:

1. anti-discrimination laws
2. affirmative action
3. equal pay for work of equal value
4. state-provided or state-subsidised childcare.

His objections are that these are a) ineffective in delivering equal opportunity, and b) not in women's best interests. While accepting much of his case, I have argued that Conway is at fault in treating these measures as a single package, and in failing to recognise important distinctions between them.

For they are *not* a single package. I personally share Conway's opposition to the fourth of these measures for the reasons given above. I share, too, his doubt about the third—equal pay legislation—not because it is unsound in principle but because it is so prone to abuse in practice. The first two measures listed, however, are not to be jettisoned so easily. Admittedly, they need careful interpretation and there are questions about how zealously or intrusively they should be applied in practice. The first of the two, affirmative action, for example, may mean no more than taking steps to encourage diversity of applicants—a policy which is, on the whole, innocuous and inoffensive. If it is taken to mean preferential treatment, however, this is a different matter. For I agree with Conway that there is no need to assume institutional or personal bias if a group is not proportionately represented in every desirable occupation or course. I agree, too, that choosing someone because she is female (though not as good as someone else who is male) is as bad as choosing someone else because he is male (though not as good as someone else who is female). Admittedly, too, it is doubtful whether women actually *need* affirmative action to progress in today's world, and true that, as a policy, it can actually harm women who achieve success through their own efforts and abilities by casting doubt on that achievement. None of these objections, however, are objections to the mere existence of anti-discrimination laws, and these represent an important public acknowledgement of a hard-won case.

Finally, it should be noted that, as Conway himself acknowledges, feminists are not a single homogeneous group. Some give a high priority to female interests, others to equality, and yet others to liberty. The question is, then, what position should the members of the third group take, i.e. feminists who set a high value on freedom? Here a striking paradox has to be recognised—that many of the freedoms sought by today's feminists turn out to be either constraints in themselves, or at least to generate other constraints. This is particularly true in areas that involve the family—marriage and cohabitation, divorce and reproduction, including reproductive medicine— in all of which areas new freedoms have had many unanticipated consequences. Very often, too, these freedoms generate costs to be paid by others—the vulnerable groups, old and young, whose well-being was on the whole protected by a secure family structure.

Nevertheless, the quest for freedom is too important to abandon lightly. The true libertarian will indeed want to avoid freedoms which generate hidden constraints for themselves or unintended costs for others, and will want also to make minimal demands, but there is no reason to exclude from this minimum the removal of formal obstacles to independence based on gender alone.

Free-Market Feminism:
A Rejoinder

Miriam E. David

T HIS essay by David Conway is beautifully written and clear in its advocacy of what he chooses to call 'free-market feminism'. It is largely a philosophical argument about the virtues of the free market for achieving and maintaining equal-opportunities feminism. This is accomplished by stating the similarities and differences between free- and anti-market feminisms, in which feminism itself is seen as having the moral high ground. There is thus no contention that feminism is good, and no discussion at all of any anti-feminist position.

The argument, therefore, hinges on his view of what the 'free market' is and in this respect is relatively simplistic. Indeed his argument is unfettered by considerations of complex historical developments in the economic, legal, political and social systems of Britain, the USA or any other advanced capitalist society. It does not give any consideration to the possibility of a changing relationship between the 'market' and the 'state' or government, in which there may be what some have called a 'mixed economy'. Here again the 'free market' is assumed to be good, and those who oppose it, or seek to constrain it, or at least its worst excesses, are then called 'anti-market' and also 'anti-capitalist' (p. 3). Thus the essayist sets up a dualism between the free-(capitalist) and anti-market (anti-capitalist) positions which I will argue is false. Moreover, he elides all the complex feminisms into one, arguing that there are just four anti-market measures or state interventions that modern feminism advocates. He then proceeds to demolish the grounds for each of these measures and tries to demonstrate that the free market (or capitalism) would serve the cause of feminism better than a regulated and constrained market.

In this reply I shall discuss the following problems with this essay, namely its definitions of feminism, markets, and their combination. I shall argue that a so-called anti-market position is one held not only by left-of-centre feminists but also by conservative feminists, and even by those left- or right-wing people who might consider themselves to be anti-feminist. In other words, I shall try to show that the arguments about the relationship between feminisms and markets in an advanced capitalist society are far more complex than those which can be reduced to a simple free- or anti-market dualism. Much of the complexity hinges not on women's role outside the family and household but on women's changing positions within families and households. It also relates more generally to developments in capitalism and therefore notions of markets, and their relationships to government and economic policies. There have been many advocates of what Conway calls the anti-market position, ranging from conservatives to social democrats to an array of feminisms, all of whom advocate some forms of state intervention/collectivism to modify and/or regulate certain markets, particularly labour markets.

What is Feminism?

To begin, however, with notions of feminism, it is perhaps best to restate the author. He offers several definitions of feminism, arguing initially that:

> [T]his species of feminism regards the market, together with the other political institutions constitutive of liberal democracy, as among the principal instruments through which the cause of female emancipation and sexual equality can be advanced ... Its roots, however, can be traced back to an earlier classical liberal form of feminism ... Its ancestry can, in turn, be traced back still earlier to the writings of John Stuart Mill and Mary Wollstonecraft (pp. 3-4).

He then goes on to further define what he takes to be the *'fundamental tenets of feminism'* as consisting of a factual claim and a closely associated value judgement that:

> as a result of having, from time immemorial up to and including the present, enjoyed less opportunity than men to participate in the extra-domestic life of their societies, women have enjoyed and continue to enjoy less esteem, status, power, and independence than men... [and] since women, in general, are no less deserving than men of enjoying such opportunity, all remaining obstacles to their enjoyment of it lack moral justification and should be dismantled (p. 5).

He adds three further points of agreement with modern feminism, namely that women have fewer legal, civil and political rights than men; second, that women continue to enjoy less opportunity than men to participate in the extra-domestic life of their societies; and third that women are more prone than men to be discriminated against from employment to educational opportunities. It is the strategies to deal with these issues that Conway claims mark the difference between the free- and anti-market feminists, namely that the latter desire the further 'curtailment of the market ... to eradicate ... discrimination' (p. 6) and the undermining 'of traditional sex roles, particularly with regard to parenting' (p. 6).

Although it appears that his definition of feminism is relatively uncontentious, albeit that he presents it in the language of traditional liberal democracy rather than that of more modernist terms, there are a number of omissions and elisions that are made. The majority of current definitions of feminisms would consider essential the notion of women's *oppression* through social as well as economic and legal or political means and measures. In other words, most modern feminists stress not only the legal, political and economic measures that serve to oppress women and thereby discriminate against them, whether in public or private, but also the concomitant social factors that may derive from social structures or social processes. Thus the argument would be that the legal, civic and political structures that may discriminate against women in favour of men simply *cannot* be viewed separately and independently of the social and economic structures and processes of societies. These too discriminate against women and may have the effect of excluding women from equal opportunities.

What is The Market?

In Conway's initial definition of feminism, however, he does curiously raise quite gratuitously the notion of the market and refer to it as if it were one institution rather than a set of mechanisms for the exchange of a whole variety of goods and services. In this respect he asserts that the so-called 'market' is on a par with his notion of feminism. This may then lead him into the more elaborated notion of feminism which is about the 'extra-domestic life of societies'. In other words, Conway confines his definition of feminism to issues in the public sphere rather than that of the private sphere of the family, which is what I assume 'domestic' to mean. He does not actually use the terms public, private or family, although he does go on to discuss parenting. In fact, he varies what he means depending upon the specific instance: '[b]y the "extra-domestic sphere" in this context is meant the realm of paid employment' (p. 16).

When he discusses the question of parenting he argues that 'anti-market feminists consider traditional sex roles ... inherently and profoundly inimical to equal opportunity for women' (p. 7). By contrast Conway believes that they are 'the result of a perfectly sensible and wholly innocuous set of complementary responses on the part of the members of both sexes to a funda-mental circumstance likely to affect their lives to an equal degree'. He goes on to argue that these different roles of mothers and fathers in the early years of parenting are perfectly compati-ble with equal opportunity in the public sphere if they are freely entered into and accepted—'fully and freely acquiesced in'. In other words he has a very narrow view of equal-opportunities feminism being about the public sphere alone which is unaf-fected and uncontaminated by lack of equality in parenting roles. This kind of view takes no account of the interrelationship between social structures and social processes and the ways in which, for instance, family structures are socially constructed rather than natural, and therefore morally good. Moreover, family and political structures, for example, are not completely separate from each other but interrelated and political decisions may have an impact upon families, and *vice versa*.

Constructing a Straw Person

Indeed, Conway develops this point as part of his critique of 'anti-market feminism'. He goes on to attack what he considers to be the recent breakdown of family life, with increasing divorce, separation and cohabitation of parents. But he argues against what might be considered to be a straw person (anti-market feminist), that it is not due to the market being inimical to women's equal opportunity but rather because of state interven-tion in social welfare. He assumes that anti-market feminists would 'blame' the market for lack of equal opportunities and thereby seek to regulate it by means of state intervention. But his own argument is based upon a similar premise that there is a relationship between the state and markets such that state intervention may 'cause' family breakdowns.

The rest of the essay is indeed an elaborate statement of this position, that state intervention has an impact upon social and familial relationships; however, it is the particular kind of impact that he wants to argue against—that it constrains rather than frees relationships. The essayist then goes on to demonstrate the inadequacies of state intervention for achieving the goals of his version of feminism, which is equal opportunities in the public sphere alone. There are four particular instances of anti-market feminism that he wishes to attack, although they happen to overlap considerably, and in essence it is the issue of equal-opportunities parenting that gives him most cause for concern. The four main measures that he 'attacks' are anti-discrimination laws, affirmative action, equal pay for work of equal value and state-provided or subsidised childcare. He takes a number of key feminists as instances of his evidence, starting with Betty Friedan and Gloria Steinem, both relatively liberal and individu-alist American feminists, as exemplars of the positions he wishes to counter, especially around the issue of childcare for young children.

For each of these measures he tries to demonstrate that by regulating or restricting employers' practices women become more rather than less disadvantaged. However, these are empirical questions and are not just subject to the force of philosophical logic. He does not adduce evidence to show that this is the case but rather argues by way of examples and particular instances. In relation to what he calls anti-discrimina-tion laws he develops a number of hypothetical case studies to illustrate the flaws in principle. Similarly, with affirmative action and equal worth he argues by example and first principle. Where he does adduce evidence he either does not cite the source or cites one which is over twenty years old:

> A substantial and growing body of evidence suggests that, in general, men are biologically equipped with a stronger drive than women to form and ascend social hierarchies. This could well account for why, in general, ... women tend to be represented in smaller numbers than men at the top of such hierarchies (p. 24).

Having asserted this incontrovertible 'evidence' he goes on later to use it without citation:

> A second alternative possible explanation of the wage gap between men and women's work is men being, in general, more motivated than women to assume positions of leadership and to strive for monetary reward, women being more concerned than men about working conditions or rewarding inter-personal aspects of their work. It is this difference which may account for the concentration of women in a comparatively restricted number of nurturant jobs (p. 30).

Moreover, he also either denies the social basis for, or disparages, the evidence. He assumes, tendentiously, that subjectivity rather than objectivity operates only for women rather than men:

> ... jobs have no intrinsic worth capable of being objectively measured. Evidence that they do not comes from the fact that job evaluation schemes used to establish the comparable worth of *women's jobs* are notoriously riddled with subjectivity and arbitrariness (emphasis added)(p. 29).

Feminism and Childcare

He reserves the main attack for his fourth form of 'state intervention', which is on early childhood care, where it is about the domestic rather than the extra-domestic life of societies. It is here that there are major sensitivities about what might be called the sexual division of labour in parenting and the different roles of mothers and fathers in relation to babies and young children. Citing two American authors and some of my own evidence, from a book written with Caroline New twelve years ago, he goes on to make the following assertion and caricatures our position as having nothing to do with social structures and processes:

> According to modern feminism, women are not as well represented as men in the highest paying and most powerful and prestigious positions in society because they are victims of sex discrimination, overt or subtle, past and present. To create equality of opportunity, so they argue, all surviving forms of discrimination against them must be eradicated, as must the baneful legacy of the past discrimination from which women have suffered. And so, the anti-market policy agenda of modern feminism is born (pp. 34-35).

Later he argues that:

> ... any couple could, if both partners chose, *decide* that, if and when they did have children, they would, quite independently of everyone

else, adopt a perfectly symmetrical division of labour between themselves, involving dual parenting and equal work, whether this be fulltime or part-time ... the decision to adopt such a form of non-division of labour between themselves would still be available to a couple in a free-market society, as would the option of their deciding that it be the father who is to assume prime responsibility for home-making and childcare and the woman prime responsibility for bread-winning (pp. 37-38).

This quotation illustrates how he has simply misunderstood the nature of our argument and that of the other writers that he takes to task about childcare. These choices are not freely available in contemporary society but are socially constructed and constrained by economic and political circumstances. However, it transpires that his concern is not with these freely available choices but rather with maintaining the traditional sexual division of parenting. He asserts quite categorically:

The *main* free-market feminist objection to state provided or subsidised childcare, then, is that it denies women the opportunity to be full-time mothers, or, at least, their primary carers, and this is what a good many of them appear to want most to be (p. 42).

In his concluding section Conway waxes quite lyrical about the virtues of a free-market society, as juxtaposed to 'state socialism' (p. 45), for ensuring equal opportunities in extra-domestic life. Indeed he goes further in finalising his assault on 'doctrinaire' (p. 44) feminists by arguing for 'lifestyle preferences' which implicitly at least is taken to mean traditional family life. It is quite clear that Conway is only a feminist in a very traditional and classical liberal sense for he ends by reserving most of his ire for those he chooses to call 'modern and post-modern feminists'. Feminism to Conway is only about the public sphere, whereas for most other feminists it is about the complex interrelationships between the overlapping and interconnected public and private spheres.

The Feminist Mistake

Christina Hoff Sommers

D AVID Conway says that a majority of contemporary feminist intellectuals 'are anti-capitalist in tone and intent'. He is right. In the United States, feminist theorists still regard modern capitalism as the prevailing system of 'patriarchal domination'.

The MacArthur Foundation, a philanthropic organisation in Chicago, annually grants a large sum of money to scholars who are deemed by their peers to be brilliant and innovative. The prize has come to be known as the 'genius award'. When Catharine Stimpson, a feminist literary theorist from Rutgers University, was named Director of the MacArthur Foundation she proceeded to award the prize to several 'geniuses' in women's studies departments. One award went to Dr. Susan McClary, a musicologist noted for her 'discovery' of rape and sexual assault themes in the symphonies of Beethoven and Mahler. Another went to the feminist economist Heidi Hartmann. Few economists have ever heard of Ms. Hartmann. Here is a sample of the kind of insight that brought her to the attention of the MacArthur Foundation:

> The struggle against capital and patriarchy cannot be successful if the study and practice of the issues of feminism is abandoned. A struggle aimed only at capitalist relations of oppression will fail, since their underlying supports in patriarchal relations of oppression will be overlooked ... While men and women share a need to overthrow capitalism they retain interests particular to their gender group.[1]

Alison Jaggar, Chair of Women's Studies at the University of Colorado, is the doyenne of American feminist philosophy. She calls herself a socialist feminist and, like Ms. Hartmann, believes that capitalism is the enemy of feminism:

> On the socialist feminist analysis, capitalism, male dominance, racism and imperialism are intertwined so inextricably, that they are inseparable; consequently the abolition of any of these systems of domination requires the end to all of them.[2]

Historically, this is nonsense. Feminism arose with the triumph of capitalism and it has flourished with the free-market system. The egalitarian ideals of the European Enlightenment and the prosperity generated by industrial capitalism provided the political and material grounds for women's emancipation. Put simply: bourgeois capitalism liberated women.

Nevertheless, objective discussions of the advantages of the market system for women are nearly impossible to find. Though few feminists outside the universities are as radical as Hartmann and Jaggar, a great many view the market with scepticism, and a large majority strongly endorse policies that place severe constraints on the workings of the free market. This includes moderates like Betty Friedan (author of the seminal *Feminine Mystique*), Eleanor Smeal (President of the Fund for the Feminist Majority), and Bella Abzug (President of the Women's Environment and Development Organization) who look with envy at socialist programmes in Sweden and Germany. It never occurs to the Friedans, the Smeals, and the Abzugs that Sweden and Germany should be emulating the United States.

Many of the political and business leaders of Europe would like nothing more than to be rid of the costly social programmes that feminists think of as 'empowering' for women. But it is nearly impossible to take back an entitlement. Europe's women are suffering from the effects of high unemployment and economic stagnation. By contrast, American women are benefiting from our low unemployment and a dynamic economy. One economist recently referred to the contemporary United States as having entered the 'Golden Age of female entrepreneurship'. French and German women are not sharing this Golden Age.

Once again, the feminists are blind to the facts. The evidence that the free market advances the cause of feminism is all around us; it is quite extraordinary that so few feminists have noticed. That is the price of the stultifying conformity that characterises feminist thought in America and England. If the feminist establishment permitted some genuine intellectual diversity (e.g. by allowing just a few conservatives, libertarians, and objectivists in the many hundreds of women's studies programmes, departments, and institutes in America and Britain) there would by now be an outpouring of books celebrating what the free market has done for women. There are no such books.

For objective assessments, one has to turn to scholarly institutes that are independent of the academy and the feminist establishment, organisations like the American Enterprise Institute, the Cato Institute, and the Heritage Foundation in the United States, and the Institute of Economic Affairs in Great Britain. Conway's 'Free-Market Feminism' is a model of the kind of scholarship and analysis that is now just beginning to surface.

A Fair Field?

Conway is a proponent of classical liberal feminism. He wants for women what classical liberals want for everyone: 'a fair field and no favours'. He is committed to increasing women's opportunities and choices. When he subjects the current feminist agenda and policies on anti-discrimination laws, affirmative action, comparable worth, and state-subsidised day care to a straightforward utilitarian analysis, he finds that these policies do more harm than good; he finds the arguments for them unpersuasive.

Consider the so-called wage gap. American feminists are fond of reminding us that women working full-time earn 72 cents for every dollar a man earns. This, they say, provides incontrovertible evidence that the market is rigged against women; it shows that programmes of affirmative action, comparable worth, and state-sponsored day care are critically needed. But the 72 cent figure is misleading. There are now millions of women (especially those in their fifties and sixties) who are working full-time, but who had stayed home for a decade or more raising children. Naturally their wages are lower than those of workers who have ten or even twenty years' seniority. When economists such as June O'Neill, head of the United States Congressional Budget Office, and Diana Furchgott-Roth of the American Enterprise Institute, take the usual relevant factors into account—education, length of time in workplace, number of hours worked per week—the wage gap comes close to disappearing.[3]

Just suppose the 72 cents on the dollar claim reflected the kind of gender bias the feminists attribute to it: that, for exactly the same work, an employer pays a man $1.00 for work a woman will do for 72 cents. Surely any number of entrepreneurs would start firing all the high-earning male employees and replacing them with women? They would then enjoy more than a 25 per cent labour cost advantage over competitors. Male workers would be driven out of the labour market in short order. That hasn't happened because the so-called gender bias pay gap is largely illusory.

As Conway points out, the discrepancy between male and female wages is the result, not of discrimination, but of the different priorities men and women have on how they balance their work and family life. 'The difference in the employment profiles of the two sexes is explicable in terms of factors other than past or present discrimination ... such as their different preferences' (p. 2). Women are far more likely than men to drop out of the workplace, or cut down on work once they have children. 'The existence of this sexual division of labour is, by itself, and without recourse to any postulated sex discrimination against women, sufficient to account for the differences between them in jobs and pay' (p. 35).

Thus, the wage gap is not due to discrimination but is the effect of men and women freely deciding to live their lives differently. Anti-market feminists criticise such preferences, complaining that they are due to a socialisation that keeps women in thrall to men. Conway denies that '*la différence*' is socially constructed. 'Unlike anti-market feminism, ... free-market feminism sees no need to dispute any of the mounting body of empirical evidence for the existence of deep-seated biologically-rooted motivational differences between the sexes which might lead couples to *choose* to divide their labour between them in ways which conform with traditional sex roles' (p. 7).

The evidence for sex differences accumulates in the most mundane places. A few years ago, Hasbro Toys, a major American toy company, tested a dolls' house they were considering marketing to both boys and girls. (The idea was not simply the result of feminist pressures; it is a matter of economics that successful unisex toys generate twice the profits of same-sex toys.) The Hasbro researchers found that girls and boys did not interact with the dolls' house in the same way. The girls dressed the dolls and played house: the boys catapulted the baby carriage from the roof. Sharon Hartley, a Hasbro general manager, came up with a novel finding: boys and girls are different.

Conway accepts the difference. There will always be far more women than men who want to stay home with children; there will always be more women than men who want to be kindergarten teachers rather than helicopter mechanics. Women and men are different: mother nature is not a feminist. For classical liberals the free market has created the best of both possible worlds. It promises equality of opportunity to everyone; and at the same time, where gender preferences hold fast, it respects them.

Totalitarian Feminism

How do the anti-market feminists respond to this kind of argument? They obdurately reject the idea that there may be natural differences between men and women determining different preferences and social roles: they keep looking to the day when boys will learn how to play with the dolls' house. (Some, on the other hand, look forward to the day when more girls will catapult the baby carriage off the roof.) They claim that 'society' is giving little girls the message that the dolls' house is their domain. They insist that women are not *freely* choosing to stay home with the children; that this so-called choice is really an artifact of sexism. They complain that men and women are still being socialised into assuming particular gender roles (e.g. women are conditioned to assume primary responsibility for children). These roles, they say, perpetuate women's subordination to men and effectively deny women equal opportunity.

This sort of argument had considerable weight at a time and place when women were uneducated and politically and economically powerless. But to suggest that women in contemporary England and America are benighted and duped into subordination is a condescending doctrine. By such arguments, says Conway, '[f]eminism goes beyond any legitimate aspiration it might have and becomes oppressive, totalitarian, and liberty-denying' (p. 8).

Simone De Beauvoir, the matron saint of second-wave feminism, gave candid expression to this authoritarian impulse some years ago during an interview with Betty Friedan. Friedan ventured the opinion that women should have the choice to stay home to raise their children if that is what they wish to do. Beauvoir disagreed:

> No, we don't believe that any woman should have this choice. No woman should be authorized to stay at home to raise her children. Society should be totally different. Women should not have that choice, precisely because if there is such a choice, too many women will make that one.[4]

De Beauvoir may have been in her Maoist phase at the time of this interview, so perhaps she held a more temperate position at other occasions. But her latter-day descendants share a common attitude towards the majority of women, who, they believe, have been socialised to make self-defeating choices. Many academic feminists still speak of women having 'false consciousness', wanting what they should not want, preferring what they should not prefer. Where the preferences are wrong, they should be thwarted.

Barbara Bergmann, a leading feminist economist from American University, recently startled some of her fellow economists (feminist and non-feminist) by opposing a long-standing proposal to include the value of non-market activity, such as housework and childcare, in the official Gross Domestic Product figures. Her reason was revealing:

> Part of the motive [of the proposal] is to lend some dignity to the position of housewives. What I think feminism is about is getting women off of the housewife track.[5]

That is not what Conway thinks feminism is about. For him, the mission of feminism is to increase choices and to increase opportunities to satisfy the preferences women actually have, not to change women's preferences by replacing patriarchal constraints with an equally limiting set of radical feminist constraints.

Consider the familiar feminist demand for full-time, affordable, high-quality, state-supported day care. Feminist theorists such as Susan Moller Okin and James Sterba believe that women's responsibility for childcare is both unfair and economically punishing. Sterba calls for state-subsidised day care as a means of 'radically restructuring' the family:

> [D]iscrimination in personal relations is the most entrenched of all forms of discrimination against women. It primarily manifests itself in traditional family structures in which the woman is responsible for domestic work and childcare ...[6]

Conway replies that in a free-market society a woman is perfectly free to make non-traditional arrangements with her spouse. Some couples choose to share domestic work and childcare; in a small number of homes the man stays home and cares for the children, and the woman works. Couples who can afford it can seek outside help. According to Conway, what Okin,

Sterba, and other feminist theorists are after is not the enhancement of women's choices: their goal is to make sure that women make choices that meet the approval of feminists of the 'right consciousness'.

Feminists rarely pause to consider the economic costs of state-subsidised day care. Conway points out that universal childcare would be awesomely expensive and would require exorbitant tax hikes. Increased taxes would inevitably force vast numbers of women into the workplace who would otherwise choose to stay at home with their children. Simone de Beauvoir might well be pleased with this result; Barbara Bergmann, Susan Moller Okin, and James Sterba may be happy that great numbers of women would be thrown off the 'housewife track'. But as Conway clearly shows, women's actual preferences would be handicapped and frustrated. The anti-market, anti-traditional-sex-role feminists would have managed to 'impose their own personal lifestyle preferences on those men and women who would prefer to live otherwise' (p. 43).

Statistical Discrimination

All the same, in opposing *all* anti-discrimination laws, Conway may be underestimating the problem posed by the sizable minority of women who want nothing to do with the 'housewife track'. It is true that women are, on average, more likely to drop out of the workplace and less physically suited to certain jobs (e.g. those that involve heavy lifting). It is also true that some women defy the stereotype and can do the same job as a man with equal ability and commitment. Yet, a rational employer, operating with imperfect information, cannot tell which women are in this sub-group. In the absence of all laws prohibiting discrimination on the basis of sex, we may expect employers to go with the odds, hiring men exclusively.

Conway is aware of this 'statistical discrimination' but he is confident that the free market will solve the problem, since qualified women will offer their services for wages lower than men's. 'Provided some enterprising employers were willing to take the risk of hiring these women for this type of work, then, once engaged in it, those women who were as or more able than men would be able to demonstrate their ability, and remove any economic incentive for an employer to discriminate against them'

(p. 19). Even so, initially, at least, many women must lose out economically. Conway does not apply his arguments against anti-discrimination laws to the case of employers who would allow racial stereotypes to determine their hiring practices, but here too it could be argued that the market solution is too long-term and that some laws prohibiting discrimination may be needed. It is, after all, a central tenet of classical liberalism that people should be judged as individuals and not as members of a group.

There may be no easy solution to the problem of statistical discrimination. I am less confident than Conway that the problem would resolve itself without at least some minimal anti-discrimination laws. On the other hand, his arguments against affirmative action, comparable worth, and state-subsidised day care are very persuasive and very much in the spirit of classical liberalism. And when he exposes the illiberal mindset of anti-market feminists, he performs a very valuable service.

The Feminism of the Future

Compare the authoritarian views of De Beauvoir with the views of a feminist contemporary who was equally famous in her day but about whom today's feminists are studiously silent. Clare Boothe Luce was a conservative feminist, which means she must be airbrushed out of history in what passes for women's studies. Luce was a successful playwright, a Republican Congresswoman from 1942 to 1946, United States Ambassador to Italy, and creator of *Life* magazine. She was an old-fashioned 'first-wave' feminist whose agenda was far removed from the kind of social engineering associated with today's anti-market feminism. As she saw it, the future was a society in which men and women were left free to work out their own arrangements:

> It is time to leave the question of the role of women in society up to Mother Nature—a difficult lady to fool. You have only to give women the same opportunities as men, and you will soon find out what is or is not in their nature. What is in women's nature to do they will do, and you won't be able to stop them. But you will also find, and so will they, that what is not in their nature, even if they are given every opportunity, they will not do, and you won't be able to make them do it.[7]

Luce assumes that nature has given women and men different propensities. She is careful to say that women's nature can only be fully known in conditions of freedom and opportunity. Notice that she has taken what is best in feminism—basic respect and fairness to women—but she has left out the intolerance and the social engineering. Luce asks for women the legal and political rights and the economic opportunities that were open to men, no less but no more. Luce's feminism was the classical liberal feminism that Conway delineates for us in the economic sphere. This is the kind of feminism a majority of men and women can comfortably embrace.

In the long run, the free market works as well for ideas as it does for goods and services. So we have good reason to expect that Conway's style of feminism is the feminism of the future.

Notes

David Conway

1   McIlroy, W. (ed.), *Freedom, Feminism and the State: An Overview of Individualist Feminism*, New York: Holmes and Meier, 1991; Kennedy-Taylor, J., *Reclaiming the Mainstream: Individualist Feminism Rediscovered*, Buffalo, N.Y.: Prometheus Books, 1992.

2   Hoff Sommers, C., *Who Stole Feminism? How Women Have Betrayed Women*, New York: Simon and Schuster, 1994.

3   For details, see Davies, S., *Libertarian Feminism in Britain, 1860-1910*, London: Libertarian Alliance, 1987.

4   Mill, J.S., *The Subjection of Women*, first published 1861, New York: Prometheus Books, 1986.

5   Wollstonecraft, M., *Vindication of the Rights of Woman*, first published 1792, Harmondsworth: Penguin Books, 1985.

6   For a review of this evidence, see Levin, M., *Feminism and Freedom*, New Brunswick, NJ: Transaction Books, 1987.

7   Conway, D., *Classical Liberalism: The Unvanquished Ideal*, Basingstoke and New York: Macmillan and St Martin's Press, 1995, pp. 56-64; and David Conway, 'Capitalism and Community', in Paul, E., Paul, J., and Miller, F. (eds.), *The Communitarian Challenge to Liberalism*, Cambridge: Cambridge University Press, 1996, pp. 137-64.

8   For further details of the evidence and argument supporting this point of view, see Murray, C., *Underclass: The Crisis Deepens*, London: IEA Health and Welfare Unit, 1994; Whelan, R. (ed.), *Just a Piece of Paper: Divorce Reform and the Undermining of Marriage*, London: IEA Health and Welfare Unit, 1995; and Morgan, P., *Farewell to the Family: Public Policy and Family Breakdown in Britain and the USA*, London: IEA Health and Welfare Unit, 1995.

9   Friedan, B., *The Feminine Mystique*, New York: W.W. Norton, 1963.

10 Friedan, B., 'Our Revolution is Unique', Mahowald, M.B. (ed.), *Philosophy of Woman*, Indianapolis: Hackett, 1978, pp. 12-19, *passim*.

11 Steinem, G., 'What It Would be Like if Women Win', in Sterba, J. (ed.), *Morality in Practice*, Third Edition, Belmont, California: Wadsworth, 1991, pp. 224-27, *passim.*

12 See Epstein, R., *Forbidden Grounds: The Case Against Employment Discrimination Laws*, Cambridge, Mass., and London: Harvard University Press, 1992.

13 For details, see *Crossing the Stage: Controversies on Cross-dressing*, Ferris, L. (ed.), London and New York: Routledge, 1993, especially the editorial introduction, pp. 1-19.

14 For a review of this evidence, see Goldberg, S., *The Inevitability of Patriarchy*, London: Maurice Temple Smith, 1977.

15 For an argument to this effect, see Conway, D., 'Does Equal Opportunities Legislation Benefit Women?', in Quest, C. (ed.), *Equal Opportunities: A Feminist Fallacy, op. cit.*, pp.53-68.

16 Brimelow, P. and Spencer, L., 'When Quotas Replace Merit, Everybody Suffers', *Forbes Magazine*, 15 February 1993, pp. 80-100. See p. 80.

17 See Sowell, T., *Affirmative Action*, Washington DC: American Enterprise Institute, 1975; and *Preferential Policies*, New York: William Morrow and Co, 1990.

18 This section is heavily indebted to two critical studies of comparable pay: Paul, E.F., *Equity and Gender: The Comparable Worth Debate*, New Brunswick, NJ: Transaction Publishers, 1989, and Rhoads, S.E., *Incomparable Worth: Pay Equity meets the Market*, Cambridge: Cambridge University Press, 1993.

19 Rector, R., quoted in Rhoads, S., *ibid.*, p. 27.

20 *Ibid*, p. 28.

21 *Ibid.*, p. 245.

22 *Ibid.*, p. 176.

23 *Ibid.*, pp. 219-20.

24 Okin, S.M., *Justice, Gender, and the Family*, New York: Basic Books, 1989, *passim*, pp. 3-17.

25 *Ibid.*, pp. 176-77.

26 Sterba, J.P., 'Feminist Justice and the Family', in Korany, J.A., Sterba, J.P. and Tong, R. (eds.), *Feminist Philosophies: Problems, Theories, and Applications*, Hemel Hempstead: Harvester Wheatsheaf, 1993, pp. 271-77, pp. 273-77, *passim.*

27 New, C. and David, M., *For the Children's Sake*, Harmondsworth: Penguin, 1985, pp. 66-77, *passim.*

28 See Morgan, P., *Who Needs Parents?*, London: IEA Health and Welfare Unit, 1996, Chapter 14.

29 Hakim, C., 'The Sexual Division of Labour and Women's Heterogeneity', *British Journal of Sociology*, Vol., 47, no. 1, March 1996, pp. 178-188. See p.179.

30 *Ibid.*, p. 181.

31 Dench, G., *The Place of Men in Changing Family Cultures*, London: Institute of Community Studies, 1996.

32 *Ibid.*, p. 19.

33 *Ibid.*, pp. 71-2.

34 Morgan, P., *The Hidden Costs of Childcare*, Wicken, Milton Keynes: Family Education Trust, 1992, pp. 43-48 *passim.*

Janet Radcliffe Richards

1 There are many modern editions of this work. Page references here are to Mill, J.S., *The Subjection of Women*, Okin, S.M. (ed.), Indianapolis: Hackett, 1988.

2 '...every established fact which is too bad to admit of any other defence, is always presented to us as an injunction of religion', (Mill, *ibid.*, p. 49).

3 *Ibid.*, p. 54.

4 *Ibid.*, p. 57 and *passim.* Note Mill's agnosticism here. He is not claiming positively that if women had the right education and opportunities they could do these things—though he undoubtedly believed that they could. He is only denying that his opponents are entitled to make their own positive claim, which they need to support their conclusion. This makes his argument much less vulnerable to attack than if he had made positive claims of his own.

5 e.g. 'What women by nature cannot do, it is quite superfluous to forbid them from doing. What they can do, but not so well as the men who are their competitors, competition suffices to exclude them from...' (*ibid.*, p. 28).

6 You might think that feminist interventions on behalf of women—the reversal of the original state of affairs—would result in its being *men* who got the unfairly small share of the unfairly small whole. But here the Conway argues that because feminist policies are often counterproductive, it will again be women who suffer.

7 *Ibid.*, pp. 1-3.

8 See e.g. Lake, 'Are we born into our sex roles or programmed into them?', Woman's Day, January 1975, pp. 24-25; and Goldberg, P., 'Are women prejudiced against women?', Transaction, 5, No. 5, pp. 28-30; quoted in Oakley, A., *Subject Women*, Oxford: Martin Robertson, p. 126.

9 Of less direct concern to markets, but presumably of long term and indirect importance, is the converse of this. The strong competition between work and children may mean that women who would have produced particularly productive children may decide not to have them.

10 Notice we cannot use what actually *has* happened as evidence here, since there have already been so many feminist interventions in the market. What follows must be understood as applying to a situation in which the woman-subjugating and women-excluding laws and institutions have been removed, but no further feminist policies implemented.

11 Consider the fates of Macintosh and Betamax.

12 Prisoners' dilemmas, obviously, and other kinds of problem whose resolution requires co-ordination and sometimes constraint.

13 Margaret Mead claimed (*Male and Female*, Penguin, 1962, p. 157) that in all known societies, what men did was regarded as more important than what women did, irrespective of what that was. When the same activities were performed by women, they were always seen as less important.

14 This would be an example of using an opponent's premises to support your own conclusion. The feminist of strong free-market inclinations does not believe anyone is intrinsically entitled to any position; her justification for wanting affirmative action, if she does, is that there are still likely to be positive obstacles to women's contributing their best for the good of all, and that these need to be removed. But when she is arguing with someone who argues on the basis of ideas of entitlement to particular jobs, she need not attack the whole idea of entitlement, even if she does think it mistaken. She can instead (or as well) argue that anyone who *does* believe in such intrinsic entitlements should recognise that at the moment the residual biases in the system mean that men are still getting jobs to which, by this criterion, they are not entitled. Such people therefore ought, on their own principles, to favour the kind of reverse discrimination that gives women a marginal preference. In fact by those standards it should probably not even count as reverse discrimination.

15 I developed arguments along these lines some time ago in *The Sceptical Feminist*, Penguin, 1980; second edition 1994, Chapter 9. Other material relevant to this essay appears in Chapter 6.

Brenda Almond

1 See Jaggar, A., 'Political philosophies of women's liberation', in Vetterling-Braggin, M., Elliston, F.A., Frederick, A. and English, J. (eds.), *Feminism and Philosophy*, New Jersey: Littlefield Adams, 1978; and Jaggar, A., *Living With Contradictions*, Boulder, Colo: Westview Press,1994.

2 These issues are discussed in a number of essays in Nicholson, L. (ed.), *Feminism /Postmodernism*, London: Routledge, 1991.

3 Russell, B., *Marriage and Morals*, London: Allen & Unwin, 1972, pp. 9-10. First published, 1929.

4 See Murray, C.,*Charles Murray and the Underclass: The Developing Debate*, London: IEA Health and Welfare Unit, 1996; and Dennis, N. and Erdos, G., *Families without Fatherhood*, London: IEA Health and Welfare Unit, second edition, 1993.

5   According to the Office for National Statistics, one quarter of all households with children are single-parent families; one third of all births are outside marriage; and 40 per cent of marriages contracted in 1994 are expected to end in divorce. *Social Focus on Families*, London: HMSO, August, 1997.

6   Rousseau, J.-J., (1762) translated in Bloom, A., *Émile, or On Education*, New York: Basic Books, 1979.

7   Wollstonecraft, M., *Vindication of the Rights of Woman*, Harmondsworth: Penguin, 1985, fist published 1792.

8   Rossi, A.S. (ed.), *Essays on Sex Equality: John Stuart Mill and Harriet Taylor Mill*, Chicago: Chicago University Press, 1970, p. 23.

9   Mill, J.S., *The Subjection of Women*, (1861) Oxford: Oxford University Press, 1975, p. 173.

10 Rossi, (ed.), *op. cit.*, p. 58.

Christina Hoff Sommers

1   Hartmann, H., 'The Unhappy Marriage of Marxism and Feminism: Towards a More Progressive Union', in Sargent, L. (ed.), *Women and Revolution*, Boston, MA: South End Press, 1981, p.32.

2   Jaggar, A., *Feminist Politics and Human Nature*, Totowa, N.J.: Rowman & Littlefied, 1988, p. 124.

3   See, for example, O'Neill, J., 'Women and Wages', *The American Enterprise*, November/December 1990, pp. 24-33; and Furchtgott-Roth, D. and Stolba, C., *Women's Figures: The Economic Progress of Women in America*, Washington, DC: Independent Women's Forum, 1996.

4   A dialogue Between Friedan and de Beauvoir, 'Sex, Society and the Female Dilemma', in *Saturday Review* June 14, 1975.

5   *Chronicle of Higher Education*, 1 December, 1993, p. A9.

6   Sterba, J.P., 'Feminist Justice and the Family', in Korany, J.A., Sterba,J.P. and Tong, R. (eds.), *Feminist Philosophies: Problems, Theories and Applications*, Hemel Hempstead: Harvester Wheatsheaf, 1993, pp.71-277. Cited in above.

7   Cited in *Reader's Digest*, June 1996.